English Accents and Dialects

An Introduction to Social and Regional
Varieties of British English

Arthur Hughes and Peter Trudgill

Edward Arnold

© Arthur Hughes and Peter Trudgill 1979

First published 1979
by Edward Arnold (Publishers) Ltd
41 Bedford Square
London WC1B 3DQ

Reprinted with corrections 1980

Hughes, Arthur
   English accents and dialects.
   1. English language—Dialects
   I. Title II. Trudgill, Peter
   427   PE1711

ISBN 0–7131–6129–9

This book is accompanied by a recording, which is available on cassette or open-reel tape.

Filmset by
Willmer Brothers Limited, Birkenhead
Printed in Great Britain by
R. Clay (Chaucer Press), Bungay, Suffolk

Contents

Acknowledgements

A very large number of people have helped us with this book, and we can acknowledge only some of them here. Over the years we have profited enormously from discussions on varieties of English with G. O. Knowles and J. C. Wells, and we are also very grateful to Peter Bedells, Viv Edwards, Sandra Foldvik, Erik Fudge, Vicky Hughes, Sandy Hutcheson, Elspeth Jones, Robin McClelland, Suzanne McClelland, James Milroy, Lesley Milroy, K. M. Petyt, and David Sutcliffe, who have provided us with information on specific points (sometimes without realizing it) and have corrected some of our worst misapprehensions. We would also like to thank all those people, many of whom went to a very great deal of trouble on our behalf, and some of whom prefer to remain anonymous, who helped us with the tape-recordings. We would particularly like to acknowledge the assistance in this respect of Gillian Brown, Ray Brown, Edwin Cannon, Joy Cannon, Chris Connor, Roseanne Cook, Karen Currie, Sally Davies, Angela Edmondson, Kirsty Evans, Anne Fenwick, Stanley Fletcher, Milton Greenwood, Wilf Jones, Chris Lawrence, Gillian Lovell, Bridie McBride, Jackie Mountford, Grahame Newell, Enid Warnes, Gwyn Williams and, especially, Euan Reid. And, finally, we are very grateful indeed to R. W. P. Brasington, J. K. Chambers, Paul Fletcher, Michael Garman, Hanne Svane Nielsen and F. R. Palmer, who read earlier versions of the book and made many valuable suggestions for improvement.

Map 1

Symbols

RP consonants

/p/	as	*p*	in	*peat*
/t/	as	*t*	in	*treat*
/č/	as	*ch*	in	*cheat*
/k/	as	*k*	in	*kite*
/b/	as	*b*	in	*bite*
/d/	as	*d*	in	*date*
/ǰ/	as	*j*	in	*jute*
/g/	as	*g*	in	*gate*
/f/	as	*f*	in	*fate*
/θ/	as	*th*	in	*thought*
/s/	as	*s*	in	*site*
/š/	as	*sh*	in	*shout*
/h/	as	*h*	in	*hate*
/v/	as	*v*	in	*vote*
/ð/	as	*th*	in	*that*
/z/	as	*z*	in	*zoo*
/l/	as	*l*	in	*late*
/r/	as	*r*	in	*right*
/w/	as	*w*	in	*wait*
/j/	as	*y*	in	*yet*
/m/	as	*m*	in	*meet*
/n/	as	*n*	in	*neat*
/ŋ/	as	*ng*	in	*long*

For RP vowels see p. 26.

Other phonetic symbols

[ʔ]	–	glottal stop
[ɫ]	–	velarized or 'dark' *l* as in RP *all*
[ɹ]	–	post-alveolar frictionless continuant as *r* in RP *rate*
[ɾ]	–	alveolar tap as *r* in Spanish *pero*
[ɻ]	–	retroflex frictionless continuant as *r* in American English *very*
[x]	–	voiceless velar fricative as *ch* in German *Nacht*
[Φ]	–	voiceless bilabial fricative
[ʍ]	–	voiceless *w*
[n̩]	–	syllabic *n* as in *hidden*
[i]	–	close front vowel as *i* in French *il*
[e]	–	half close front vowel as *e* in French *été*
[a]	–	open front vowel
[ɑ]	–	open back vowel
[ɔ]	–	half open back rounded vowel as *o* in French *fort*
[o]	–	half close back rounded vowel as *au* in French *haut*
[u]	–	close back rounded vowel as *ou* in French *tout*
[ø]	–	half open front rounded vowel as *eu* in French *peu*
[ɨ]	–	close central vowel
[ʉ]	–	close central rounded vowel
[ɵ]	–	half close central rounded vowel, between [ø] and [o]
[ɐ]	–	half open central vowel, resembles *u* in RP *but*
[ɪ]	–	central vowel more open than [i] and more central than [ɪ]

Vowel charts

To indicate the quality of vowels, we make use in the text of cardinal vowel charts. For the reader unfamiliar with this system, a fair idea of how it works can be had from comparing the quality of RP vowels with the positions assigned to them in figures 4.1 to 4.3. A vowel is assigned a position on two dimensions: open v close, and front v back, and this position corresponds roughly to the position in the mouth of the highest point of the tongue in the production of that vowel. Presence or absence of lip rounding is shown by choice of symbol. Diacritics are used to give more precise indication of vowel quality. For a fuller account of the cardinal vowel system, see O'Connor (1973).

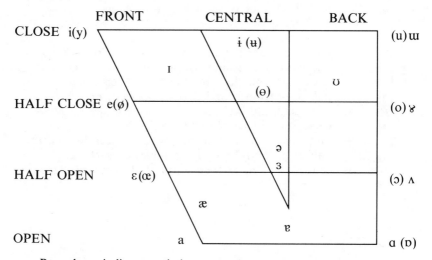

Parentheses indicate symbols representing vowels with lip rounding

Diacritics
   ⊤ more open
   ⊢ retracted
   ¨ centralized
   : long
   . half long
   ' stress

1

Variation in English

When the foreign learner of English first comes to the British Isles, he is usually surprised (and dismayed) to discover how little he understands of the English he hears. For one thing, people seem to speak faster than he expected. For another, the English that most of them speak seems to be different in many ways from the English he has learned. While it is probably differences of pronunciation that will immediately strike him, the learner may also notice differences of grammar and vocabulary.

His reaction to this experience will vary. If he is confident in his own and his teachers' ability, he may conclude that most of the English (and Welsh, Scottish, and Irish) people that he hears cannot, or at least do not, speak English correctly. In this he would find many native speakers to agree with him. Indeed, there would even be some who would tell him that, since he has *studied* the language, he should know better than they what is correct.

We shall deal in two ways with this suggestion that native speakers cannot speak their own language correctly. Firstly, we can point out that for the learner visiting Britain the question of correctness is largely irrelevant. His problem is to understand what he hears, regardless of whether it is correct or not. And the description and analysis of variation provided in this book, together with the tape recordings, is an attempt to help him do this. They should also help him decide which features of what he hears he can safely integrate into his own speech. The second thing we can do is to try to show that the notion of 'correctness' is not really useful or appropriate in describing the language of native speakers. We shall not do this immediately, but when examples of what might be considered incorrect English arise.

Another reaction on the part of the learner to his failure to understand what is said may be to think that perhaps what he learned in his own country was not 'real' English. Happily, nowadays this is unlikely to be the case. But, although the English he has learned is real enough, it will tend to be limited to a single variety of the language, one chosen to serve as a model for his own speech. It will usually be the speech of a particular group of native speakers as it is spoken, slowly and carefully, in rather formal situations. Given limitations of time, of teachers' knowledge, and of students' aspirations and attitude, this restriction is entirely reasonable, at least as far as speaking is concerned. The learner, though he may sound somewhat odd at times, will usually be able to make himself understood. But such a restriction as far as listening comprehension is concerned is less easily justified. While the native speaker may be able to 'decode' the learner's message, he does not generally have the ability, or the inclination, to 'encode' his own message in a form comprehensible to the learner. In many cases, of course, he will simply not be aware of the difficulty. Even when he is, his most common strategy will be to repeat what he has just said, only louder, or to revert to 'foreigner talk' (me come, you go–savvy?), usually making understanding even more difficult. It seems to us, therefore, that exposure to a number of varieties of English, and help in understanding them, can play an important and practically useful part in the study of English as a foreign language.

Even when the learner with comprehension problems recognizes that English, like his own language, indeed like every language, is subject to variation, so complex and at times so subtle is that variation that it is usually a long time before he begins to see much order in it. And native speakers, even those who teach the language, are often hard put to explain the things that puzzle him. For this reason, we shall attempt now to give some idea of the principal ways in which British English speech varies and, just as important, the non-linguistic factors which condition that variation. It is hoped by doing this to provide a framework in which to set the features of social and regional variation, which will be our main concern in the remainder of the book, and to show how they are related to other types of variation.

Variation in pronunciation

RP

We must first make clear the way we are going to use two important terms, 'dialect' and 'accent'. We shall use DIALECT to refer to varieties distinguished from each other by differences of grammar and vocabulary. ACCENT, on the other hand, will refer to varieties of pronunciation. The reason for making this distinction will become apparent as the chapter proceeds.

Whenever British rather than, say, American English is taught, the accent presented as a model for the learner will almost always be 'received pronunciation', or 'RP'. 'Received' here is to be understood in its nineteenth-century sense of 'accepted in the best society'. While British society has changed much since that time, RP has nevertheless remained the accent of those in the upper reaches of the social scale, as measured by education, income and profession, or title. It is essentially the accent of those educated at public schools (which are of course private, and beyond the means of most parents). It is largely through these schools that the accent is perpetuated. For RP, unlike prestige accents in other countries, is not the accent of any region (except historically: its origins were in the speech of London and the surrounding area). It is quite impossible to say from his pronunciation where an RP speaker comes from.

It has been estimated that only about three per cent of the English population speak RP (see Trudgill, 1979). Why, then, is it the accent taught to foreign learners? Its prestige has already been mentioned. No doubt learners want to learn, and teachers to teach, the 'best' accent, and for most British people, because they associate the accent with the high social status of its speakers, RP is the best and even the most 'beautiful' accent. There is another reason, however, for learning RP. If we were asked to point to a readily available example of RP, we would probably suggest the speech of BBC newsreaders. Because of its use on radio and television, within Britain RP has become the most widely understood of all accents. This in turn means that the learner who succeeds in speaking it, other things being equal, has the best chance of being understood. Another good reason for learning RP is that it is by far the most thoroughly described of British accents. This is the case, at least in part, because descriptions of it were made in response to the needs of foreign learners and their teachers.

Language change

The learner who has been presented with RP as a model should not think, when he comes to Britain, that speech he hears which is in some way different from that model is necessarily not RP. First, accents, like all components of living languages, change with time. In RP, for example, there is a tendency at present for certain triphthongs and diphthongs to become monophthongs. Thus the word *tyre*, which was once most commonly pronounced /taiə/ (triphthong), came to be pronounced /taə/ (diphthong), and is now increasingly reduced to /ta:/ (monophthong, with the same pronunciation as the word *tar*). These changes with time can be seen reflected to some degree in the pronunciation of speakers of different ages. Young people, most particularly those of the highest social class and educated at the most prestigious public schools, will tend to say /ta:/ (advanced RP); those somewhat older will tend to say /taə/ (general RP); and there will be others, older still, who will say /taiə/ (conservative RP). Of course there is not a perfect correlation between age and pronunciation. Some RP speakers, including the young, will regard the distinguishing features of the advanced variety of the accent as 'affected' and not alter their own speech, at least not until with the passage of time the adoption of these features becomes more general. Other RP speakers will be only too ready to integrate them into their own speech. Which variety of RP is taught will differ from country to country, indeed from classroom to classroom. What the learner of advanced RP should bear in mind is that this form of pronunciation does sound affected to most British people, and that, if he acquires it successfully, even though his listener is aware that he is a foreigner, his speech may sound affected too. For many people with regional accents all RP speech, however conservative, sounds affected, and the supposed affectation is felt most strongly at those points where the differences between RP and the regional accent of the listener are most marked. (See chapter 3 for further discussion of RP.)

Stylistic variation

As we have just seen, there are differences of pronunciation among RP speakers. There is, in addition, variation in the pronunciation of an individual RP speaker. Most trivially, studies in instrumental phonetics have shown that a person cannot produce even a single sound in exactly the same way twice in succession. And it is obvious that someone with food in his mouth, or who has just drunk eight pints of beer, will not speak in quite the same way as in other circumstances. But what is more significant for us are the changes in pronunciation made, consciously or unconsciously, by a speaker according to his perception of the situation in which he finds himself, especially how formal or informal he feels it to be. His judgement of formality will depend on a number of factors, such as the relative status of the person he is talking to, how well they know each other, what they are talking about, to what purpose and in what place. Some idea of the range of formality can be given by listing just a few of the terms for occasions on which words are uttered— proclamation, lecture, consultation, conversation, chat. In what the speaker sees as a very formal situation he will tend to articulate more slowly and carefully. Individual sounds will be given their full value; none will be omitted. In a very informal situation, on the other hand, he will be more likely to speak quickly, less carefully, and some sounds will either have their value changed or be omitted entirely. Thus the word *are* may be pronounced /ɑː/ in deliberate speech, but (when unstressed) will become /ə/ in more casual speech (this process being known as vowel weakening); /ðæt pleit/ (*that plate*) will become /ðæp pleit/ (assimilation); /ɪkspˈɛkt souː/ (*expect so*) will become /ɪkspˈɛk souː/ (elision). Variation conditioned in this way by a person's perception of the situation in which he is speaking we refer to as 'stylistic'.

It should not be thought that a more casual style of pronunciation is in any sense incorrect. It is really not a matter of correctness, but of appropriateness. It would be odd, even ridiculous, for a radio commentator to use the same style of pronunciation when telling his girlfriend how desirable she is, as when describing for his listeners a royal procession. It is just possible nevertheless that there are radio commentators who would do this, for it is not only situational factors which determine style of pronunciation, but also the speaker's personality. Some people are very sensitive to what they regard as the demands of a situation on their speech style, while others appear indifferent, speaking with little change of pronunciation in the widest range of situations. Some of those who always speak carefully and with great deliberation maintain that to do anything else is slovenly, sloppy, and leads to loss of clarity and to possible misunderstanding. In this claim they forget how much of language is redundant. There is usually far more information in an utterance than we need in order to understand it. The small loss in information resulting from modifications in pronunciation of the kind exemplified above rarely causes confusion: /ɪksp'ɛk sou/ can only be *expect so*. Even where linguistically there is ambiguity, the situation will normally disambiguate: if we are asked if we would like some /mɪns/, we can infer without too much difficulty from the proffered rattling bag that the offer is of *mints* and not *mince* (meat). And if we were not sure, in an informal situation it would be perfectly natural to ask which was intended.

As has been said before, whatever the learner thinks about this kind of thing, his task is to understand what is said. Unfortunately, it is a task for which he is not always well prepared. Language teachers, like all of us, want to be understood, and are inclined to speak slowly and with deliberation, a tendency in which they are not discouraged either by their students or by the often formal atmosphere of the classroom. The learner may be familiar with such processes as vowel weakening, assimilation and elision, but he usually has little idea of the degree to which they occur in ordinary conversational English. Even the tape recorded conversations of native speakers marketed commercially tend to sound rather stiff and stilted. The need for recordings of speech of a more spontaneous nature has been recognized, however, and these are becoming available (Crystal and Davy, 1975).

Unconditioned variation

Within RP there are differences of pronunciation which cannot be explained in terms either of a change taking place or of speech style. Examples are the pronunciation of *economic* as /iːkən'ɒmɪk/ or /ɛkən'ɒmɪk/. Speakers will have a preference for one over the other, and all that we can usefully say is that some people, perhaps a majority, say this and others say that.

Regional variation

As we have seen, only a very small percentage of the population speak RP. The others have some form of regional accent. Much of chapter 3 is concerned with regional accents, and we shall do no more here than make some general observations.

Regional accents are sometimes spoken of as, for instance, northern or southern English, Irish, or Welsh. But this is not to say that there is, for example, one Irish or one north of England accent. It means only that speakers in one of those areas, say the north of England, have enough pronunciation features in common with each other, which are not shared with speakers of other areas, for us to say of someone we hear speaking, 'He's from the north.' Just as 'northern accent' is no more than a convenient label for a group of more local accents, something like 'Yorkshire accent' is simply a label for a group of accents which are even more local. Almost however small an area we look at, we will find differences between the pronunciation there and an area adjoining it. At the same time, unless there is some considerable obstacle to communication between the two areas, those differences will be so slight that we should be unhappy about drawing a line between them and saying that on one side of the line the accent was X and that on the other it was Y. From the southwest of England to the north of Scotland we do not have a succession of distinct accents, but a continuum, a gradual changing of pronunciation. In order to describe regional variation, however, it is convenient at times to speak of accents as if they were entities to be found within certain well defined limits, and from now on this is what we shall do.

Speakers of RP are at the top of the social scale, and their speech gives no clue to their regional origin. People at the bottom of the social scale speak with the most obvious, the 'broadest' regional accents. Between these two extremes, in general (and there are always individual exceptions) the higher a person is on the social scale, the less regionally marked will be his accent, and the less it will differ from RP. This relationship between class and accent can be represented diagrammatically in the form of a triangle:

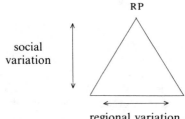

RP

social
variation

regional variation
in pronunciation

This relationship between accent and the social scale can be illustrated with figures for 'aitch-dropping' (say, for example, /æt/ instead of /hæt/) in the Bradford area of Yorkshire (Petyt, 1977):

	% aitches dropped
Upper middle class	12
Lower middle class	28
Upper working class	67
Middle working class	89
Lower working class	93

Not all people stay in one social position throughout their lives. Those who climb the social scale will tend to modify their accent in the direction of RP, thereby helping to maintain the existing relationship between class and accent. A speaker with a Bradford accent would begin to pronounce more aitches. He might try, too, to introduce the vowel /ʌ/, absent from northern English accents but which in RP distinguishes *putt* /pʌt/ from *put* /pʊt/. But to do this is not easy. It means dividing all those words which in the north of England contain the vowel /ʊ/ into two groups according to their pronunciation in RP. What often happens is that some words which have /ʊ/ in RP as well as in the regional accent are wrongly classified, and so *cushion* /kˈʊšṇ/ in both accents, is pronounced /kˈʌšṇ/. This is referred to as hypercorrection (see p. 28).

In view of what has just been said, it is not surprising that there seems to be greater variation in the speech of the individual speaker of modified regional accents than in that of RP speakers. In what he regards as a formal situation, particularly in the company of RP speakers, he will probably not only attempt to make his speech more like RP, but, since he is effectively a learner of RP, he will also speak more slowly and carefully in order to avoid making mistakes.

It is sometimes said that nowadays there is not the same pressure as there once was to modify one's speech in the direction of RP. Reference is made to the fact that announcers with non-RP accents are now to be heard on the BBC, that important posts in industry and the civil service are held by non-RP speakers, and that some younger RP speakers have adopted, more or less deliberately, features of regional pronunciation. Perhaps the pressure is less, but it is still there. In a recent experiment carried out in south Wales, a university lecturer, introduced as such, gave the same talk, word for word, to two matched groups of schoolchildren aged 16 to 18 years (Giles *et al.*, 1975). The only difference between the two talks was the accent. He addressed one group in RP, the other in a Birmingham accent. When the schoolchildren were then asked to evaluate the lecturer according to a number of criteria, those who had heard him speak RP gave him a significantly higher rating on intelligence than the group who had heard him use a Birmingham accent. It is true that some people appear most unwilling, despite changes in their social status, to modify their regional accent, and that certain regional accents (including some Scottish) are more prestigious and felt to require less modification than others. It is probable, however, that, if only by contact with more RP speakers, there is some modification of pronunciation attendant on social advancement.

Grammatical and lexical variation

Standard English

The term ACCENT, as we have seen, refers to varieties of pronunciation. The term DIALECT, on the other hand, at least as we shall use it here, refers to varieties distinguished from each other by differences of grammar and vocabulary. With British English, though not with all other languages, the separation of accent from dialect is not only logically possible but almost required by the relationship that holds between them. The accent taught to foreign learners of British English is RP. The dialect used as a model is known as 'standard English', the dialect of educated people throughout the British Isles. It is the dialect normally used in writing, for teaching in schools and universities, and heard on radio and television. Unlike RP, standard English is not restricted to the speech of a particular social group. While it would be odd to hear an RP speaker consistently using a non-standard dialect of English, most users of standard English have regional accents. What social variation there is within standard English appears to be limited to a rather small number of lexical items, the choice of the word *serviette* rather than (table) *napkin*, for example, indicating inferior social standing.

Another way in which standard English differs from RP is that it exhibits some regional variation. Subsumed under standard English (better, standard British English) are standard English English (in England and Wales), standard Scottish English, and standard Irish English. In Scotland and Ireland there are regional features which, because they are to be found regularly even in formal writing, are considered 'standard'. In standard Scottish English, for example, we find 'They hadn't a good time' rather than the standard English English, 'They didn't have a good time.' It goes without saying that it is usually the latter which is taught to foreign students. Variation between these standard dialects is in fact quite limited, and should cause the learner no problems.

Language change

The grammar of a dialect changes with time, but very slowly.

Grammatical forms and structures, members of tightly knit, closed systems, resist alteration, and it is not easy to identify ongoing grammatical development.

One interesting example of grammatical variation which may represent the beginning of a change in the language is the apparently increasing use of the 'present perfect' in conjunction with expressions of definite past time reference. One hears such things as, 'And Roberts has played for us last season' (without any kind of break). Most native speakers, it must be admitted, would find this odd. They would claim that the speaker had made a mistake. But sentences like this are heard more and more often. The captain of a cricket team who said, 'And Roberts has played for us last season', had been asked about the present strength of his side. His answer combined an indication of the current relevance of Roberts's having played with the information that it was in the previous season that he had played. In this way he said in one sentence what can normally only be said in two: 'Roberts has played for us. He played last season.' It is not at all certain that the use of this grammatical device will continue to increase. For the time being it will be regarded as a mistake. But if eventually it becomes generally accepted (just as previously 'incorrect' sentences like 'The house is being built next spring' are now accepted as good English), then it will be yet another subtlety for the foreign learner to master, in an area which is already difficult enough.

Lexical change is more rapid than grammatical change. It is easier to see the variation that sometimes accompanies it. In some cases a new lexical item enters the language and displaces one already there. In this way *record player* has largely taken the place of *gramophone*, which is heard mostly in the speech of older people.

In other cases, an established lexical item begins to change its meaning, or take on a second meaning. The word *aggravate*, for instance, which not long ago meant exclusively 'make worse', is now often used to mean something like 'irritate', as in 'That man aggravates me.' There are some people (who write to newspaper editors) who argue that since *aggravate* is derived from the Latin *aggravare*, which has the meaning 'make worse', then that must be the true meaning of *aggravate* in English. But if this argument were applied generally, it would suggest that the real meaning of *nice*, since it is derived from the Latin *nescius*, is 'ignorant'.

There are other people who argue that giving a second meaning to *aggravate* could lead to misunderstanding. This is hardly likely, as in its first sense the verb requires an abstract object, while in its second sense it requires an animate object. For the moment, most educated people avoid using *aggravate* to mean 'irritate'. The foreign learner, while recognizing the possibility of a second meaning for *aggravate* (and for other words that are changing, as well), should probably do the same.

Stylistic variation

A person's choice of grammatical structure and vocabulary will vary with the situation in which he is speaking. On a formal occasion someone might say 'the person to whom I wrote', while less formally he might say 'the chap I wrote to'. One phrase is not more correct than the other. Despite the protestations of pedants, there is no reason, except custom, why words called 'prepositions' should not end sentences. What happened to be the case in Latin is not necessarily the case in English. And the word *chap* is in no way inferior to the word *person*. Likewise, swear words and slang are not wrong in themselves. Again, as with the features of pronunciation discussed earlier, it is a matter not of correctness, but of appropriateness.

When even highly educated people are chatting together with friends, their speech is very different from textbook conversations. They begin a sentence, then change their mind; they hesitate, then start again, differently; they muddle one grammatical structure with another. They omit various words, forget others, replacing them with *thingy* or *wotsit*; if necessary they will invent words just for the occasion. In a relaxed atmosphere they do not feel constrained to speak carefully, to plan what they are going to say. This makes understanding difficult for the learner, of course. But once account is taken of his difficulties, when people begin to speak more carefully, inevitably the atmosphere changes somewhat.

Regional variation

Standard English, we have said, is a dialect. There are many other, regional dialects in Britain, which differ from standard English in various ways. There are grammatical differences. So, in East Anglia the third person singular present tense is not marked with an *s*. We find *he go*, *he eat* instead of standard English, *he goes*, *he eats*. There are differences, too, of vocabulary. What is known as a *clothes horse* in standard English and southern dialects is called a *maiden* in northern dialects.

Not everybody speaks the dialect of the area he belongs to. There is a relationship between social class and dialect similar to the one between social class and accent. The higher a person's position on the social scale, the less his speech is regionally marked. This can be exemplified with the figures from a survey carried out in Norwich (which is in East Anglia). The number of third person singular present tense verb forms without *s* were counted and then expressed as a percentage of all third person singular present tense verb forms. The results for various social groups were as follows (Trudgill, 1974):

	% forms without *s*
Upper middle class	0
Lower middle class	29
Upper working class	75
Middle working class	81
Lower working class	97

In British schools great efforts are made by teachers to eradicate features of local dialect from the speech and, more particularly, the writing of their pupils. The teachers tend to think of these regional features as mistakes in standard English. Usually they are not very successful in their efforts. It is true that the longer a child stays at school, and the more successful he is, the less regionally marked, grammatically and lexically, will be his speech. But, as length of stay and success at school themselves correlate highly with social class, this may not be very significant. It is true, however, that some people do modify their speech quite considerably. In many cases they can be regarded as having two dialects, speaking standard English in certain company and their local dialect (often with a more regional accent than they usually affect) in other company. In this way they make a claim to belong to more than one social group.

Correctness

We have mentioned the idea of correctness on a number of occasions already in this chapter. We want here just to summarize briefly what we have said. Three types of things are often said to be incorrect.

First, elements which are new to the language. Resistance to these seems inevitable, but almost as inevitable, if they prove useful, is their eventual acceptance into the language. The learner needs to recognize these and understand them. It is interesting to note that resistance seems weakest to change in pronunciation. There are linguistic reasons for this, but in addition the fact that in RP innovation is introduced by the social elite must play a part.

Second, features of informal speech. This we have argued is a matter of style, not correctness. It is like wearing clothes. There is nothing wrong, at least in our eyes, in wearing a bikini, but it is a little out of place at a dinner party (but no more than a dinner jacket would be for lying on the beach). In the same way, there are words one would not normally use when making a speech which would be perfectly acceptable in bed, and vice versa.

Third, features of regional speech. We have said little about correctness in relation to these, because we think that once they are recognized for what they are, and not thought debased forms of the prestige dialect or accent, the irrelevance of the notion of correctness will be obvious.

Summary

The most prestigious British dialect is standard English; the most prestigious accent is RP. It is with these that the learner is most familiar. What he is not usually so familiar with, however, is the degree of variation to be found within standard English and RP. This variation, part of it stylistic, part of it attributable to changes in the language, is not the subject matter of this book (but see the section on further reading). Nevertheless, it is important that the learner should be aware of its existence, and not mistake it for the social and regional variation with which we are principally concerned.

Standard English is not the dialect of any social group, but of educated people throughout the British Isles. Nevertheless, most people in Britain (including those who would generally be regarded as speakers of standard English) have at least some regional dialect forms in their speech. In general, the higher a person is on the social scale, the fewer of these regional forms his speech will exhibit. The main ways in which regional dialects differ from standard English are outlined in the next chapter.

RP is not the accent of any region. It is spoken by a very small percentage of the British population, those at the top of the social scale. Everyone else has a regional accent. The lower a person is on the social scale, the more obvious his regional accent will tend to be. Differences between RP and regional accents are discussed in chapter 3.

2

Dialect Variation

In this book we cannot provide a comprehensive list of all the grammatical differences to be found between non-standard British dialects and standard English. We can, however, describe some of the forms most common in urban varieties, and point out the *type* of differences to be looked for in each area. We shall do this, briefly, in this chapter. Further examples, together with instances of lexical variation, will be cited in the individual sections of chapter 4.

Multiple negation

There are some grammatical forms which differ from those in standard English and which can be found in most parts of the country. This is because, in these cases, it is in fact the standard dialect which has diverged from the other varieties.

A good example of this is the grammatical construction well known throughout the English-speaking world as 'the double negative'. If we take a sentence in standard English such as:

    I had some dinner

we can note that there are two different ways of making this sentence negative. We can either negate the verb:

    I didn't have any dinner

or we can negate the word *some*, by changing it to *no*:

    I had no dinner

These sentences do have different stylistic connotations, the latter being more formal, but they mean approximately the same thing.

The main point is that in standard English one can perform one or other of these operations, but not both. In most other English dialects, however, one can do both these things at once. The result is 'multiple negation':

    I didn't have no dinner

(Linguists prefer the terms *multiple negation* or *negative concord* to the more common 'double negative' since this construction is not limited to two negatives. It is possible to have three or more: *She couldn't get none nowhere.*)

It is safe to say that constructions of the type *I didn't have no dinner* are employed by a majority of English speakers. (At one time this construction was found in the standard dialect, too, and it has parallels in many other languages. It is often, however, considered to be 'wrong' by many people in the English-speaking world. This is largely because it is, like most non-standard grammatical forms, most typical of working-class speech, and for that reason tends to have low prestige. People who believe it to be 'wrong', we can say, are probably making what is ultimately a social rather than linguistic judgement.)

On the other hand, there is considerable regional variation in the type of constructions in which multiple negation is permitted. The following sorts of construction occur in some non-standard dialects but not in others:

> *We haven't got only one* (=Stand. Eng. *We've only got one*)
> *He went out without no shoes on*

Other aspects of negation in non-standard dialects

The form *ain't* is not found throughout Britain, as is multiple negation, but is nevertheless extremely common. It is variously pronounced /eint/, /ɛnt/, or /ɪnt/, and has two main functions. First, it corresponds to the negative forms of the present tense of *be* in standard English, *aren't*, *isn't, am not*:

> *I ain't coming*
> *It ain't there*
> *We ain't going*

Secondly, it functions as the negative present tense of auxiliary *have*, corresponding to standard English *haven't, hasn't*:

> *I ain't done it*
> *He ain't got one*

Note, however, that it does not usually function as the negative present of the full verb *have*:

> **I ain't a clue*
> *I haven't a clue*

(The asterisk indicates an unacceptable construction.)

The form *aren't* also occurs more widely in non-standard dialects than in standard English. In standard English, of course, it occurs as the negation of *are* as in *we aren't, you aren't, they aren't*. It also occurs in the first person singular with the interrogative *aren't I?*. But in some non-standard dialects the form *I aren't*, equivalent to standard English *I'm not*, also occurs. (*I amn't* occurs in parts of the West Midlands and Scotland.)

In most Scottish dialects, negation is formed not with *not*, but with *no* or its more typically Scottish form *nae* /ne/. Thus we find forms in Scottish English such as:

He's no coming
I've nae got it
I cannae go

Past tense of irregular verbs

Regular verbs in English have identical forms for the past tense and for the past participle, as used in the formation of perfect verb forms:

Present	Past	Present perfect
I work	I worked	I have worked
I love	I loved	I have loved

Many irregular verbs, on the other hand, have in standard English distinct forms for the past tense and past participle:

Present	Past	Present perfect
I see	I saw	I have seen
I go	I went	I have gone
I come	I came	I have come
I write	I wrote	I have written

In many non-standard dialects, however, there is a strong tendency to bring the irregular verbs into line with the regular, the distinction being signalled only by the presence or absence of *have*. There is considerable regional variation here, but in some cases we find the original past participle used also as the past tense form:

Present	Past	Present perfect
I see	I seen	I have seen
I come	I come	I have come

(In this last case, as with *hit, put, cut* etc. in standard English, all three forms are identical.) In other cases levelling has taken place in the other direction:

Present	Past	Present perfect
I go	I went	I have went

And in others the present tense form may be generalized:

I see	I see	I have seen
I give	I give	I have give

We can also note common forms such as:

I write	I writ	I have writ

and the continuation of the historical tendency to make irregular verbs regular:

I draw	I drawed	I have drawed

The verb *do* is also involved in social dialect variation of this type, and in a rather interesting way. As is well known to learners of English as a foreign language, *do* has two functions. It can act as a full verb, as in:

He's doing maths at school
I did lots of work

And it can also act as an auxiliary verb, and is used as such in interrogation, negation, emphasis, and 'code' (Palmer, 1974):

> *Did you go?*
> *You went, did you?*
> *We didn't go*
> *I did like it*
> *We went and so did they*

In standard English, the forms of the full verb and of the auxiliary are identical:

> *He does maths, does he?*
> *You did lots of work, didn't you?*

In most non-standard dialects, however, the full verb and the auxiliary are distinguished in the past tense, as the full verb has been subjected to the levelling process described above, while the auxiliary has not. That is, the past tense form of the full verb is *done*, that of the auxiliary *did*:

> *You done lots of work, didn't you?*
> *I done it last night. Did you? Yes I did.*

These non-standard dialects therefore have a grammatical distinction that is not found in the standard dialect.

NEVER as past tense negative

In non-standard dialects in most parts of the country, the word *never*, in contrast to standard English, can refer to a single occasion, and functions in the same way as the form *didn't*. Thus *I never done it* means 'I did not do it' with reference to a single, particular occasion. Forms of this type are particularly common in the speech of children, but are well attested in adult speech too:

> *She did yesterday, but she never today*
> *You done it! I never!*

Present tense verb forms

The present tense form of the verb in standard English is somewhat anomalous in that the third person singular form is distinguished from the other forms by the presence of –*s*:

> *I want*
> *you want*
> *we want*   but   *he, she, it wants*
> *they want*

In a number of non-standard dialects, this anomaly is not found. In East Anglia (as in many American varieties), this verb paradigm is completely regular as a result of the absence of the third singular –*s*. In these dialects, forms such as the following are usual:

She like him
It go very fast
He want it
He don't like it

The individual form *don't*, in fact, is very common indeed throughout the English speaking world in the third person singular.

In other parts of Britain, including parts of the north of England and especially the south west and south Wales, the regularity is of the opposite kind, with –*s* occurring with all persons of the verb:

I likes it
We goes home
You throws it

In parts of the west of England this leads to the complete distinction of the full verb *do* and auxiliary *do*:

	Present	*Past*	*Past participle*
Full verb:	dos	done	done
Auxiliary:	do	did	—

Thus:

He dos it every day, do he?
He done it last night, did he?
(*Dos* is pronounced /duːz/.)

In other dialects, including many in Scotland and Northern Ireland, the forms with –*s* in the first and second persons and in the third person plural are a sign of the 'historic present', where the present tense is used to make the narration of past events more vivid:

   I go home every day at four o'clock
but   *"I goes down this street and I sees this man hiding behind a tree . . ."*

Cf. I says in narration (at least in folk American speech)

Relative pronouns

In standard English, *who* is used as a relative pronoun referring to human nouns, *which* for non-humans, and *that* for nouns of both types. The relative pronoun is also very frequently omitted in restrictive relative clauses where it refers to the object of a verb:

That was the man who did it	*That was the man who I found*
That was the man that did it	*That was the man that I found*
	That was the man I found
That was the brick which did it	*That was the brick which I found*
That was the brick that did it	*That was the brick that I found*
	That was the brick I found

These forms are also found in non-standard dialects, but a number of additional forms also occur, including omission of pronouns referring to the subject:

That was the man what done it
That was the man which done it
That was the man as done it

> *That was the man at done it*
> *That was the man done it*

The form with *what* is particularly common. Possessive relatives may also differ from standard English:

> *That's the man what his son done it*
> cf. Stand. Eng.   *That's the man whose son did it*

Reflexive pronouns

The reflexive pronouns in standard English are formed by suffixing *–self* or *–selves* to

(a) the possessive pronoun:

my	*myself*
your	*yourself*
our	*ourselves*

(b) the object pronoun:

him	*himself*
it	*itself*
them	*themselves*

(The form *her + self herself* could be regarded as being based on either the possessive or the object pronoun.)

Many non-standard dialects have regularized this system so that, for instance, all forms are based on the possessives:

myself	*herself*
yourself	*itsself*
hisself	*ourselves*
	theirselves

Comparatives and superlatives

Standard English permits comparison through either the addition of *more:*

> *She's more beautiful than you*

or through the addition of *–er:*

> *He's nicer*

Many non-standard dialects permit both of these simultaneously:

> *She's more rougher than he is*

The same is also true with superlatives. Since Shakespeare wrote *The most unkindest cut of all* this form has been lost in standard English, but survives in many other dialects:

> *He's the most roughest*

Demonstratives

Corresponding to the standard English system of:

this	*these*
that	*those*

a number of social and regional variants occur. Most commonly, standard English *those* corresponds to *them* (sometimes, particularly in Scottish dialects, *they*) in non-standard dialects:

> *Look at them animals!*
> *Look at they animals!*

In the north of England and Scotland, the form *yon* (cf. *yonder*) also occurs, often as part of a more extended system in which *yon* refers to objects more distant than those referred to by *that*:

this	*these*
that	*them*
yon	*yon*

Adverbs

In standard English, there are many pairs of formally related adjectives and adverbs:

> *He was a slow runner*   *He ran slowly*
> *She was a very clever speaker*   *She spoke very cleverly*

In most non-standard dialects, these forms are not distinct:

> *He ran slow*
> *She spoke very clever*
> *They done it very nice*
> cf. *He'll do it very good*

In the case of some adverbs, forms without *–ly* are also found in colloquial standard English:

> *Come quick!*

although some speakers might not accept this as standard English.

Unmarked plurality

A very widespread feature indeed is that, after numerals, many nouns of measurement are not marked for plurality, in many non-standard dialects:

> *a hundred pound*
> *thirteen mile*
> *five foot*

Three inch, however, does not seem to occur.

Prepositions of place

Prepositions exhibit a large degree of variation in their usage in British dialects. This is particularly true of prepositions of place, and we can do no more here than cite a very few examples of cases where non-standard dialects can differ from standard English:

> *It was at London* (=*It was in London*)
> *He went up the park* (=*He went to the park*)
> *I got off of the bus* (=*I got off the bus*)

Lexical features

We shall be dealing further with variation in vocabulary in individual sections. It is worth noting here, however, that some features such as the lack of distinction between *teach* and *learn*, and between *borrow* and *lend*, are found in nearly all non-standard dialects:

> *They don't learn you nothing* (=*They don't teach you anything*)
> *Can I lend your bike?* (=*Can I borrow your bike?*)

Features of colloquial style

At some points it is difficult (as we saw above in the case of the example *Come quick!*) to distinguish between features of colloquial style and those of non-standard dialect. The following are a few of these:

(a) *us* can function as the first person singular object pronoun:

> *Give us a kiss!*

(b) pronoun apposition—a personal pronoun immediately following its antecedent noun:

> *My dad he told me not to*

(c) indefinite *this*: *this* can function as an indefinite article, particularly in narratives:

> *There's this house, see, and there's this man with a gun*

Variation within standard English

The standard English dialect itself is subject to a certain amount of variation. Some of this is regional: educated people in different parts of Britain do vary to a certain extent in the way in which they speak, and even write, English. (These differences normally involve features which are also found in the regional non-standard dialects.) And some of it is to do with age: as we saw in chapter 1, all languages and dialects change, and standard English is no exception.

1   Speakers of standard English in the south of England tend to use contracted negatives of the type:

> *I haven't got it*
> *She won't go*
> *Doesn't he like it?*

The further north one goes, the more likely one is to hear the alternative type:

> *I've not got it*
> *She'll not go*
> *Does he not like it?*

This is particularly true of Derbyshire, Lancashire (apart from Liverpool which, as we shall see, is in a number of ways linguistically as southern as it is northern), Cumbria and Scotland. In Scotland forms of this type are almost invariably used. Elsewhere, it is more a matter of tendencies than of absolute rules. Southern speakers (see above) use the northern-type contraction in *I'm not*, since *I amn't* does not occur in standard English. They also quite frequently use the *you're not, we're not, they're not* forms rather than the more typically southern-type forms with *aren't*. Part of the reason for this may lie in the stigmatized non-standard usage of this form with the first person singular, *I aren't*.

2 In most grammatical descriptions of standard English it is stated that the indirect object precedes the direct object:

> *She gave the man a book*
> *She gave him it*
> *She gave him the book*

If the preposition *to* is employed, however, then of course the direct object can precede:

> *She gave a book to the man*
> *She gave it to him*
> *She gave a book to him*
> *She gave it to the man*

In the south of England, the forms with *to* seem to be the most common, particularly where the direct object is a pronoun. However, in the educated speech of people from the north of England, other structures are also possible:

(a) *She gave it him* is very common indeed, and is also quite acceptable to many southern speakers;

(b) *She gave it the man* is also very common in the north of England, but is not found in the south;

(c) *She gave the book him* is not so common, but can be heard in the north of England, particularly if there is contrastive stress on *him*;

(d) *She gave a book the man* is not especially common, but does occur in northern varieties, particularly again if *man* is contrastively stressed.

3 There are regional differences in which participle forms are used after verbs such as *need* and *want*:

Southern England:	*I want it washed* *It needs washing*
Parts of Midlands and northern England:	*I want it washing* *It needs washing*
Scotland:	*I want it washed* *It needs washed* ↓

4 There are a number of regional and age-group differences in the use of the verbs *must* and *have to*. These can be demonstrated with reference to table 2.1.

The forms in the (b) 'negative modal' column have the meaning 'He is

cf. Albanian <u>duhet lavë</u> and Rumanian <u>trebuie spălat</u>.

Table 2.1: *must* and *have to* in southern English English

	(a) Positive	(b) Negative modal	(c) Negative main verb
Non-epistemic	(i) He must do it He has to do it He's got to do it	He doesn't have to do it He hasn't got to do it	He mustn't do it
Epistemic	(ii) He must be in		He can't be in
Non-epistemic	(iii) He had to do it He'd got to do it	He didn't have to do it He hadn't got to do it	
Epistemic	(iv) He must have been in		{ He couldn't have been in He can't have been in
	(v) He'll have to do it	He won't have to do it	

not compelled to do it (but he can if he likes)' etc., while the forms in the (c) 'negative main verb' column have the meaning 'He is compelled not to do it'. The 'epistemic' uses (rows (ii) and (iv)) are those where inferences are being drawn: 'It is certain that he is in (because I can hear his radio)' etc. It can be seen that in standard English in the south of England (the variety most often described in grammar books) only *must* appears in (c) and only *have to* or *have got to* in (b). It will also be seen that (iiic) and (vc) are blank: there is no way of saying 'He must not do it' in the past or future: one has to use constructions such as 'He wasn't allowed to do it'. In the north of England, however, these gaps are filled. At (ic), in these areas, it is possible to have *He hasn't to do it* (and, for some speakers, *He's not got to do it* or *He hasn't got to do it*—which are therefore ambiguous in a way they are not in the south of England) with the additional meaning *He mustn't do it*. Similarly, with the past, (iiic), educated northern English can have *He hadn't to do it* (as well as *He didn't have to do it* and *He hadn't got to do it* or *He'd not got to do it*, which are again ambiguous). And in the future, (vc), northern speakers have *He'll not have to do it* or *He won't have to do it* (which are ambiguous) and even *He'll haven't to do it*.

At (iic) and (ivc) the usual northern forms are *He mustn't be in* and *He mustn't have been in*. And for many younger speakers, in both the north and the south, probably as the result of North American influence, *have to* and *have got to* have also now acquired epistemic use, particularly in positive, present tense usage. Thus *He must be the greatest player in the world* can now also be *He's got to be the greatest player in the world* or *He has to be the greatest player in the world*.

5 It is possible to divide English verbs into two main classes according (among other criteria) to whether or not they employ auxiliary *do* in negatives and interrogatives:

He walked	*He didn't walk*	*Did he walk?*
She laughed	*She didn't laugh*	*Did she laugh?*
She can leave	*She can't leave*	*Can she leave?*
He will go	*He won't go*	*Will he go?*

Verbs of the second type come into the category of modals and auxiliaries.

(a) The verbs *ought to* and *used to* are often described in English grammars as coming into this second category, and indeed are employed in this way by some older speakers:

He ought not to go	*Ought he to go?*
They used not to go	*Used they to go?*

With younger speakers, however—and this is particularly true of the interrogative form, especially with *used to*—these verbs are being reclassified in the first category:

He didn't ought to go	*Did he ought to go?*
They didn't use to go	*Did they use to go?*

(b) In some cases the verb *have* is clearly an auxiliary, used in the formation of perfect verb forms, and operates as such:

> *You've been there*   *You haven't been there*   *Have you been there?*

In other cases it is quite clearly not an auxiliary, and takes *do*:

> *He has his lunch at home*   *He doesn't have his*   *Does he have his lunch at*
>   *lunch at home*   *home?*

There are a number of cases, however, where the status of *have* is variable, and where there is considerable regional and age-group variation. This variation is further complicated by the *have got* construction, and by differences between tenses. Table 2.2 shows the various possibilities in different varieties.

Table 2.2:   *have* in modern English

		1	2	3	4	5 (USA)
(a)	Have you been there?	1	1	1	1	1
	Had you been there?	1	1	1	1	1
(b)	Have you any money?	1	1	0	0	0
	Have you got any money?	1	1	1	1	0
	Do you have any money?	0	0	0	1	1
(c)	Had you any money?	1	1	0	0	0
	Had you got any money?	1	1	1	1	0
	Did you have any money?	1	1	1	1	1
(d)	Have you a good time?	0	0	0	0	0
	Do you have a good time?	1	1	1	1	1
(e)	Had you a good time?	1	0	0	0	0
	Did you have a good time?	1	1	1	1	1
(f)	Have you your lunch at home?	0	0	0	0	0
	Do you have your lunch at home?	1	1	1	1	1
(g)	Had you your lunch at home?	?	0	0	0	0
	Did you have your lunch at home?	1	1	1	1	1

1 = occurs

0 = does not occur

Column 1 gives the usage typical of perhaps most Scottish and Northern Irish speakers; column 2, the usage of many northern (particularly Lancashire, but not Liverpool), and older southern English speakers (as described by Palmer); column 3, the colloquial usage of most younger southern English speakers; column 4, the usage of certain younger educated British speakers, particularly in formal styles—which may show American influence; and column 5, shows typical North American usage. It will be seen that American usage treats *have* as a normal verb except where it is clearly an auxiliary, and that this is also possible in all varieties of British English with the past form. (In the present tense, it is only possible with habitual meaning, as in (d) and (f).) In British English there is greater freedom for *have* to be treated as an auxiliary, however, particularly with Scottish, northern and older southern English speakers. Where the *got* form is not available (where no element of possession is indicated) it is only the Scottish variety which permits the auxiliary-type treatment, and here only with the past form. Scottish, Irish and some northern English varieties also treat *have* more like an auxiliary in that they permit contraction where many English varieties do not:

Scottish and Irish:	*He'd a good time last night*
English and Welsh:	*He had a good time last night*

6 It is well known that certain verb-particle constructions in English ↓ have alternative forms as follows:

    (a) *He turned out the light*
         Put on your coat!
         She took off her shoes

    (b) *He turned the light out*
         Put your coat on!
         She took her shoes off

There is, however, regional variation with respect to this usage in Britain. All speakers will accept both (a) and (b) as normal English, but speakers in the south of England are more likely to employ the (b) forms in their own speech, whereas Scottish speakers almost invariably use forms of type (a).

↓ A 17-year old man (Studs Terkel programme on Chicago's WFMT, 6 May 1983) : "... to come more and more out. ...To come out more and more." He corrected himself probably because of the possible ambiguity in his original utterance.

3

Accent Variation

As we have already seen, the accent of British English which has been most fully described, and which is usually taught to foreign learners, is the accent known as RP. Since many descriptions are therefore available (see, for example, Gimson, 1980) we will not give any detailed description of RP here. (Table 3.1, however, does illustrate the symbols used in this book for the vowels of RP.)

In this chapter we shall, first, give a very brief outline of some of the differences currently to be found, largely as a result of age-group differences, within RP. Then the bulk of the chapter will be devoted to describing the main regional differences to be found in non-RP accents of British English and to comparing them with RP. We do not attempt to give a detailed account of all the regional and social differences in pronunciation to be found in British English. In particular, we do not attempt at all to describe accents spoken by older people in rural areas (for these, see Wakelin, 1972). Rather we concentrate on urban and other regional accents of the type which are most widely heard as one travels round the country, and which are most likely to be encountered by foreign visitors. More detailed discussion of phonological features takes place in chapter 4. Intonational and other prosodic features are not dealt with, but can of course be noted from the tape.

Differences within RP

In addition to the vowels shown in table 3.1, older RP speakers have the vowel /ɔə/ in words such as *more, pore*, which are thereby distinguished

Table 3.1: the vowels of RP

pit	/ɪ/	bee	/iː/	beer	/ɪə/
pet	/ɛ/	bay	/ei/	bear	/ɛə/
pat	/æ/	buy	/ai/	bird	/ɜː/
put	/ʊ/	boy	/ɔi/	bard	/ɑː/
putt	/ʌ/	boot	/uː/	board	/ɔː/
pot	/ɒ/	boat	/ou/	poor	/ʊə/
		bout	/au/		

from *maw, paw* which have /ɔ:/. Younger speakers, on the other hand, are losing the /ʊə/ vowel of *poor*, and are beginning to merge pairs such as *moor* and *more*, *poor* and *pore*, so that the original three-way distinction has been lost altogether:

	paw	*pore*	*poor*
older speakers	/ɔ:/	/ɔə/	/ʊə/
middle-aged speakers	/ɔ:/	/ɔ:/	/ʊə/
younger speakers	/ɔ:/	/ɔ:/	/ɔ:/

In a series of similar developments, the vowel /ɛə/ of *there, pear* is becoming monophthongal /ɛ:/ and the triphthongs /aiə/ as in *fire* and /auə/ as in *power* are becoming simplified to /a:/ (as noted in chapter 1). This particularly true of the single word *our*, which large numbers of RP and non-RP speakers now pronounce /a:/ even though they may retain /auə/ in other words such as *hour* and *flower*.

A further feature which differentiates the conservative speech of older RP speakers from that of younger speakers involves the pronunciation of words such as *off, lost, froth*. We know that originally words of this type had the same short /ɒ/ vowel as words like *hot, top*. At some stage, however, a change took place in southern English accents (including RP) such that /ɒ/ became lengthened to /ɔ:/ before the voiceless fricatives /f/, /s/, /θ/(for the parallel development of /æ/ to /a:/, see below). During this century, however, this innovation has been reversed, and the original short vowel pronunciation is being restored. This restoration appears to have been led particularly by middle-class speakers, with the result that pronunciations such as *off* /ɔ:f/, *lost* /lɔ:st/, *froth* /frɔ:θ/ are now most typical of lower status working-class accents and, within RP, of older-fashioned more conservative or aristocratic speakers. If, therefore, a speaker says *off* /ɔ:f/ rather than /ɒf/ he is likely to be older rather than younger, and upper middle class or working class rather than lower middle class.

Regional accent differences

1   *The vowel* /ʌ/

(a) One of the best known differences between British English accents is one of phoneme inventory—the presence or absence of particular phonemes. Typically, the vowel /ʌ/ does not occur in the accents of the north and Midlands of England, where /ʊ/ is to be found in those words that elsewhere have /ʌ/. The vowel /ʌ/ is relatively recent, in the history of English, having developed out of /ʊ/, and northern accents have not taken part in this development. The result is that pairs of words such as *put: putt, could: cud* which are distinguished in Welsh, Scottish, Irish and southern English accents are not distinguished in the north and Midlands, where words like *blood* and *good, mud* and *hood*, are perfect rhymes. (There are a few common words, though, which have /ʌ/ in the south of England but which have /ɒ/ in most of the north of England. These include *one*, which rhymes with *on* in these areas, *tongue*, and *none*.)

Many northern speakers, under the influence of RP, have a vowel which is between /ʊ/ and /ʌ/ in quality in words such as *but* (and sometimes in words such as *put* also). Generally, this vowel is around [ə] (see table 3.2). This is particularly true of younger, middle-class speakers in areas of the southern Midlands. (Some speakers too, of course, hypercorrect—see chapter 1.)

We can also note that many (particularly older) northern speakers, while they do not have /ʌ/, do have /uː/ rather than /ʊ/ in words such as *hook, book, look, took, cook*. They therefore distinguish pairs such as *book* and *buck*, which in the south are distinguished as /bʊk/ and /bʌk/, as /buːk/ and /bʊk/. (All English English accents have shortened the original long /uː/ in *oo* words to /ʊ/ in items such as *good, hood*; and all seem to have retained /uː/ in words such as *mood, food*. But in other cases there is much variation. RP speakers may have either /uː/ or /ʊ/ in *room, broom*; eastern accents have /ʊ/ rather than /uː/ in *roof, hoof*: western accents, as well as those from parts of Wales, may have /ʊ/ rather than /uː/ in *tooth*; and so on.)

(b) It is usual, in descriptions of RP, to consider /ʌ/ and /ə/ as distinct vowels, as in *butter* /bˈʌtə/. This also holds good for accents of the south-east of England, and Scotland. However, speakers from many parts of Wales, western England, and the Midlands (as well as some northern speakers—see above) have vowels that are identical in both cases: *butter* /bˈətə/, *another* /ənˈəðə/ (see table 3.2).

Table 3.2:   /ʌ/, /ʊ/ and /ə/

	but	*put*
RP	/ʌ/	/ʊ/
Northern	/ʊ/	/ʊ/
Western; modified northern I	/ə/	/ʊ/
modified northern II	/ə/	/ə/
hypercorrect northern	/ʌ/	/ʌ/

2   /æ/ and /ɑː/

Another very well known feature which distinguishes northern from southern English accents concerns the vowels /æ/ and /ɑː/. In discussing this feature we have to isolate a number of different classes of words:

(i)	*pat, bad, cap*	RP /pæt/ etc.
(ii)	*path, laugh, grass*	RP /pɑ:θ/ etc.
(iii)	*dance, grant, demand*	RP /dɑ:ns/ etc.
(iv)	*part, bar, cart*	RP /pɑ:t/ etc.
(v)	*half, palm, banana, can't*	RP /hɑ:f/ etc.

RP has /æ/ in set (i), and /ɑː/ in all other sets. This incidence of vowels in the different sets is also found in all southeastern English accents. In the Midlands and north of England, on the other hand, words in sets (ii) and (iii) have the vowel /æ/ rather than /ɑː/, although they do have /ɑː/ in the classes of (iv) and (v). Thus, whereas southerners say /grɑːs/ *grass*, /grɑːnt/ *grant*, northerners say /græs/ and /grænt/. (Normally /æ/ is pronounced [a] in most northern areas.)

This difference between the north and south of England is due to the fact that the original short vowel /æ/ was lengthened (cf. the lengthening of /ɒ/ to /ɔː/ above), in the south of England (a) before the voiceless fricatives /f/, /θ/, /s/; and (b) before certain consonant clusters containing an initial /n/ or /m/. Change (a) affected most words in southern English accents. Exceptions include words such as: *daffodil, gaff, Jaffa, raffle, Catherine, maths, ass, crass, gas, hassle, lass, mass, chassis, tassel*, which have /æ/ in RP, and southern accents. There are also some words which vary: some southerners have /æ/ in *graph, photograph, alas*, others have /ɑː/.

Change (b) is rather more complex and less complete. We can note the following phonological contexts, and typical southern English pronunciations:

	/ɑː/		/æ/
– nt	*plant*	but	*pant*
– ns	*dance*	but	*romance*
– nš†	*branch*	but	*mansion*
– nd	*demand*	but	*band*
– mp	*example*	but	*camp*

†Many speakers actually have č rather than š here.

(Words such as *transport, plastic* can have either /æ/ or /ɑː/.)

Some Welsh accents (like many Australian accents) have change (a) but not change (b): they have /grɑːs/ *grass* but /dæns/ *dance*.

This discussion of the incidence of /æ/ and /ɑː/ in words like *grass* and *dance* is not relevant to Scottish and Irish accents (except for some RP influenced accents—some middle-class Edinburgh speakers, for example). These accents do not have the vowel /ɑː/, and therefore have /æ/ not only in sets (i), (ii) and (iii), but also in sets (iv) and (v). (The /æ/ may be pronounced [æ], [a] or [ɑ] in these varieties.) They do not, that is, have any contrast between pairs such as *palm: Pam, calm: cam.*

This is also true of those accents most typical of the southwest of England (see map 2). RP speakers in this area do, of course, have the /æ/:/ɑː/ contrast, as do many other middle-class speakers whose accents resemble RP. But speakers with more strongly regional southwestern accents do not have the contrast, or at most have a contrast that is variable or doubtful. It is certain that southwestern accented speakers have /æ/ (often pronounced [a·]) in words of classes (i), (ii) and (iii). (For class (iv), see below.) The doubt lies in what these speakers do with

Map 2

A = /æ/ in *path*
B = /ɑ:/ in *path*
C = /æ/-/ɑ:/ contrast absent or in doubt

words of set (v). Typically, it seems, words such as *father, half, can't* have /æ/. Words such as *palm, calm* retain the /l/, and generally have /ɒ/:/pɒlm/. More recent loan words like *banana, gala, tomato*, which have /ɑ:/ in southeastern and northern English accents and /æ/ in Ireland and Scotland, most typically have /æ/ but *may* have /ɑ:/, and are even pronounced [təmˈɑ:ɹtou] etc. by some western speakers.

3 /ɪ/ *and* /i:/

Another major north-south differentiating feature involves the final vowel of words like *city, money, coffee* (as well as unstressed forms of *me, he, we*). In the north of England (as in RP) these items have /ɪ/:/sˈɪtɪ/*city*. In the south of England, on the other hand, these words have /iː/:/sˈɪti./. The dividing line between north and south is in this case a good deal further north than in the case of the previous two features, only Cheshire, Lancashire and Yorkshire and areas to the north being involved—except that, again, Liverpool is in this case southern rather than northern. Tyneside, too, has /iː/ rather than /ɪ/.

This is the only major feature in which RP agrees with northern rather than with southern English regional accents.

Scottish accents typically have the same vowel in this final position as they have in words such as *gate, face*: e.g. *hazy* [hˈeze].

4 /r/

Most English accents permit /r/ where it occurs *before* a vowel, as in *rat, trap, carry*. They vary, however, in whether they permit the pronunciation of /r/ after a vowel ('post-vocalic' /r/), as in words such as *bar* and *bark*. RP does not have post-vocalic /r/ and has *bar* /bɑː/, *bark* /bɑːk/. Scottish and Irish accents (like most North American accents) do have /r/ in this position.

Within England and Wales the position of post-vocalic /r/ in regional accents is quite complex, but we can generalize and say that the pronunciation with /r/ is being lost—post-vocalic /r/ is dying out—and that one is more likely to hear post-vocalic /r/s in the speech of older, working-class rural speakers than from younger middle-class urban speakers. Map 3 shows those areas where post-vocalic /r/ still occurs in urban speech.

This difference between English accents is due to a linguistic change involving the loss of post-vocalic /r/, which began some centuries ago in the southeast of England, and has since spread to other regions. This loss of /r/ has also had a further consequence. The consonant /r/ was lost, in these accents, before a following consonant, as in *cart,* but *not* before a following vowel, as in *carry*. This meant that whether or not the /r/ was pronounced in words like *car* depended on whether it was followed by a word beginning with a vowel, or by a word beginning with a consonant (or by a pause). Thus we have:

	car engine	with /r/	/kɑːrˈɛnʤɪn/
but	*car port*	without /r/	/kɑː pɔːt/

The /r/ in the pronunciation of *car engine* is known as 'linking r'. Originally, we can assume, what happened was that you *deleted* (or failed to pronounce) the /r/ before a following *consonant*. Subsequently, however, this pattern has been restructured, analogically, for most speakers, so that it is now interpreted in such a way that you *insert* an r before a following *vowel*. This means that analogous to:

soar /sɔː/   soar up /sɔːr ʌp/
we now also have
    draw /drɔː/   draw up /drɔːr ʌp/
Where r occurs in this position—where there is no r in the spelling (the spelling reflects the original pronunciation, of course)—it is known as 'intrusive r'. Because there is no r in the spelling, intrusive /r/ has often been frowned upon by school teachers and others as being 'incorrect'. However, it is now quite normal in those accents of English which are 'r-less', and even in RP it is quite usual for speakers to say:
    idea of   Shah of Persia
    draw it   India and
and other such phrases with an /r/. We can say that where one of the vowels /ɑː/, /ɔː/, /ɜː/, /ɪə/, /ɛə/, /ə/ occurs before another vowel, an /r/ is automatically inserted. Indeed this process is so automatic that speakers are usually unaware that they do it. Generally, too, we can say that the tendency is now so widespread that if a speaker with a southeastern-type English accent fails to use intrusive /r/, especially after /ə/ or /ɪə/, he is very probably a foreigner. Many RP speakers, however, are careful not to use intrusive /r/ *within* words, and will not say *drawing* /drɔːrɪŋ/, as many other non-RP speakers do.

Accents such as Scottish accents which have preserved post-vocalic /r/ do not, of course, have intrusive /r/ (the analogical process does not apply), and Scottish speakers often observe that 'English speakers say *India* /ɪndɪər/'. English speakers, in fact, do not say /ɪndɪər/ but they *do* say /ɪndɪər ən pɑːkɪstɑn/ *India and Pakistan.*

Loss of post-vocalic /r/ in RP and many other accents also means that many words, such as *butter, better, hammer*, end in –/ə/ (rather than –/ər/). When many new words such as *America, china, banana, algebra* were adopted into the English language, there was in these accents therefore no problem. They fitted into the same pattern and were pronounced with final /ə/—(with intrusive /r/, of course, if the next word began with a vowel). However, in accents where post-vocalic /r/ was preserved, there were no words ending in –/ə/, and the problem therefore arose of how to incorporate these new words into the English sound structure of these particular varieties. In many Scottish accents the solution seems to have been to end words such as these with /æ/ (the same vowel as in *hat*): /čʼainæ/ *china.* In accents in the west of England, on the other hand, another solution was sometimes adopted and the new words assimilated to the pattern of *butter*. We therefore find, in towns such as Southampton, pronunciations such as /bən'ænər/ *banana*, /vən'ɪlər/ *vanilla* and so on. (This is not the same phenomenon as intrusive r, because in these accents the r occurs even where there is a following consonant.) And in Bristol the solution was to assimilate them to the pattern of *bottle, apple* /ˈæpəl/. This is the so-called 'Bristol l' (see p.47), as in *America* /əmˈɛrɪkəl/, *Eva* /ˈiːvəl/, and so on.

Map 3

A = post-vocalic /r/ present
B = post-vocalic /r/ absent

5 */u:/ and /ɔ:/*

We have already noted that Scottish and Northern Irish accents have no distinction between /æ/ and /ɑ:/. The same is also true, for the most part, of the similar pairs of vowels /ʊ/ and /u:/, and /ɒ/ and /ɔ:/. Thus Scottish speakers make no distinction between pairs of words such as the following:

Pam	:	*palm*
pull	:	*pool*
cot	:	*caught*

6 /h/

Unlike RP, most urban regional accents in England do not have /h/, or are at least variable in its usage. For these speakers, therefore, *art* and *heart*, *arm* and *harm*, are pronounced the same. Speakers in the northeast of England, including Newcastle, do however retain /h/, as do Scottish and Irish speakers.

7 [ʔ]

RP speakers may use the glottal stop word-initially before vowels: *ant* [ʔænt]; or before certain consonants or consonant clusters: *batch* [bæʔč], *six* [sɪʔks], *simply* [sɪmʔplɪ] (Brown, 1977).

In most regional accents, however, the glottal stop is more widely used, particularly as an allophone of word-medial and word-final /t/. It is most common in the speech of younger urban working-class speakers, and is found in most regions, with the particular exception of many parts of Wales. It occurs much more frequently in some phonological contexts than others:

most frequent	*that man*	– finally before a consonant
	button	– before a syllabic nasal
	that apple	– finally before a vowel
	bottle	– before a syllabic /l/
least frequent	*better*	– before a vowel

(In the *that man* context, the glottal stop can also be heard from many RP speakers.)

In some areas, especially the northeast of England, East Anglia, and Northern Ireland, the glottal stop may also be pronounced simultaneously with the voiceless stops /p/, /t/, /k/ in certain positions, most strikingly when between vowels:

flipper	[flˈɪpʔə]
city	[sˈɪtʔiː]
flicker	[flˈɪkʔə]

8 /ŋ/

(a) Most non-RP speakers of English, particularly in informal styles, do not have /ŋ/ in the suffix *–ing*. In forms of this type they have /n/ instead:

singing	/sˈɪŋɪn/
walking	/wˈɔːkɪn/

This pronunciation is also stereotypically associated with older members of the aristocracy, who are often caricatured as being particularly interested in 'huntin', shootin', and fishin''.

(b) In an area of western central England which includes Birmingham,

If this statement is correct, then ŋ → n must have spread through analogy from the verbal -ing (participating) to the nomina

Manchester and Liverpool, words which elsewhere have /ŋ/ and are spelt *ng* are pronounced with [ŋg]:

singer	[sɪŋgə]
thing	[θɪŋg]

9   /j/–*dropping*

At an earlier stage in the history of the English language, words like *rude* and *rule*, it is thought, were pronounced /rju:d/, /rju:l/. In modern English, however, the /j/, where it occurred after /r/, has been lost, and the pronunciation is now /ru:d/, /ru:l/. The same thing is true of earlier /ju:/ after /l/: words such as *Luke*, which formerly had /j/, are today pronounced /lu:k/ (except that some—particularly Scottish—accents still preserve /j/ in words like *illumine, allude*). Currently, too, /j/ is being lost after /s/: most speakers have *super* /s'u:pə/, but many still retain /j/ in *suit* /sju:t/, for example. In RP and many other English accents, though, this is as far as the process has gone, and /j/ can still occur before /u:/ after all other consonants. In certain regional accents, however, the change has progressed a good deal further. In parts of the north of England, for example, /j/ has been lost after /θ/, so that *enthuse* may be /ɛnθu:z/. In London, /j/ is very often lost after /n/: *news* may be /nu:z/ rather than RP-type /nju:z/. (And, as in a number of North American accents, /j/ can also, at least in northern areas of London, be lost after /t/ and /d/: *tune* /tu:n/, *duke* /du:k/, rather than /tju:n/, /dju:k/ as in RP.) In a large area of eastern England, however, /j/ has been lost before /u:/ after *all* consonants. This area covers Norfolk and parts of Suffolk, Essex, Cambridgeshire, Northamptonshire, Bedfordshire, Leicestershire, Lincolnshire and Nottinghamshire, and includes the towns of Norwich, Ipswich, Cambridge and Peterborough. In this area pronunciations such as *pew* /pu:/, *beauty* /b'u:ti:/, *view* /vu:/, *few* /fu:/, *queue* /ku:/, *music* /m'u:zɪk/, *human* /h'u:mən/, are quite usual.

-ing) —unlike what happened in some other varieties of English, where one is shootin' ~~animals~~ (ŋ > n), but where the shooting of the animals does not show this ŋ > n. After all, the /ŋ/ ≠ /n/ contrast is alive in all (?) of English (rang/ran, thing/thin). (How about ~~somethin'~~, etc., though?)

4

British Accents and Dialects

In this chapter we are going to look in greater detail at the speech of ten different areas of the British Isles. These correspond to the ten recordings of conversations on the tape which is made available with the book. The speakers on the tape have quite distinct accents, and have been chosen to provide a sample of regional variation which is linguistically and geographically representative. The towns from which the speakers come are: London (the speech and the speakers being known as 'cockney'); Norwich (East Anglia); Bristol (the west of England); Pontypridd (south Wales); Walsall (West Midlands); Bradford (Yorkshire); Liverpool (Merseyside); Newcastle (the north east); Edinburgh (Scotland); Belfast (Northern Ireland). The locations of these towns are shown on map 1 (p. vii).

We shall treat each area in turn, indicating first the principal distinguishing features of the particular accent, and making reference where possible to examples of them in the recording (identified by line number in the transcript, e.g. 1.10). Then follows an orthographic transcription of the relevant recording, and notes on interesting grammatical and lexical features which appear in the recording.

We should point out here, perhaps, that the recordings were not made by actors or in a studio. For the most part they are of people talking with friends in their own homes. In order to obtain speech which was natural, we wanted them to feel comfortable and relaxed, to speak as they usually would in friendly conversation. We think that in general we have achieved this. The conditions in which the recordings were made does mean, however, that there are occasions when people get excited, are interrupted, turn away from the microphone, or rattle a teacup in its saucer, and for this reason it is not always possible to decide just what is being said.

The recording for each area begins with the reading of a word list which is designed to bring out the principal differences between British accents. For comparison, the very first recording on the tape is of an RP speaker reading that list. The list, together with the RP pronunciation of it, is given in table 4.1 (and is referred to subsequently as WL, with the number identifying the word, e.g. WL 5).

Table 4.1: the word list used in the recordings

1 pit /pɪt/	19 city /sɪtɪ/	36 fur /fɜ:/
2 pet /pɛt/	20 seedy /si:dɪ/	37 fair /fɛə/
3 pat /pæt/	21 hat /hæt/	38 nose /nouz/
4 put /pʊt/	22 dance /dɑ:ns/	39 knows /nouz/
5 putt /pʌt/	23 daft /dɑ:ft/	40 plate /pleɪt/
6 pot /pɒt/	24 half /hɑ:f/	41 weight /weɪt/
7 bee /bi:/	25 father /fɑ:ðə/	42 poor /pʊə/
8 bay /beɪ/	26 farther /fɑ:ðə/	43 pour /pɔ:/
9 buy /baɪ/	27 pull /pʊl/	44 pore /pɔ:/
10 boy /bɔɪ/	28 pool /pu:l/	45 paw /pɔ:/
11 boot /bu:t/	29 pole /poul/	46 tide /taɪd/
12 boat /bout/	30 Paul /pɔ:l/	47 tied /taɪd/
13 bout /baʊt/	31 doll /dɒl/	48 pause /pɔ:z/
14 beer /bɪə/	32 cot /kɒt/	49 paws /pɔ:z/
15 bear /bɛə/	33 caught /kɔ:t/	50 meet /mi:t/
16 bird /bɜ:d/	34 fir /ɜ:/	51 meat /mi:t/
17 bard /bɑ:d/	35 fern /fɜ:n/	52 mate /meɪt/
18 board /bɔ:d/		

Note that the RP speaker on the tape is relatively young and therefore has (WL 15) *bear* /bɛ:/ and (WL 42) *poor* /pɔ:/ (see p. 27).

In the sections that follow we shall repeatedly want to speak about the qualities of different vowels. For example, in Cockney, although the vowel /ʌ/, as in *cup*, is to be found in the same set of words as it is in RP, its realization (i.e. the actual sound made) is consistently different. To show these differences (which, of course, can be heard on the tape) we shall make use of vowel charts. To allow comparisons, typical realizations of the monophthongs and diphthongs of RP are given in figures 4.1, 4.2 and 4.3.

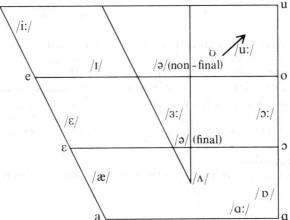

Figure 4.1 Typical realizations of RP monophthongs

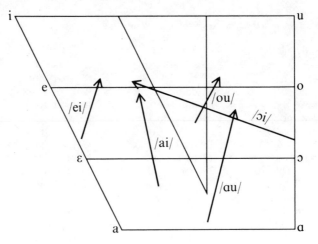

Figure 4.2 Typical realizations of RP rising diphthongs

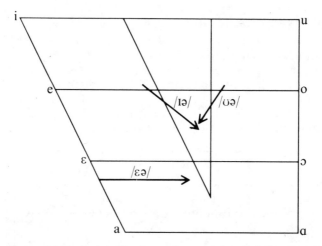

Figure 4.3 Typical realizations of RP centring diphthongs

I London

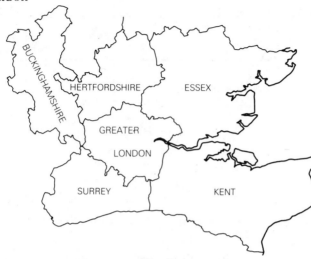

Map I

1 Cockney is, of course, a southern accent.
  (a) /ʊ/ and /ʌ/ are both present and distinguish between, for example, *put* and *putt* (WL 4, 5; see p. 27). /ʌ/ is realized as [æ⊢] (figure 4.4), a clear example being *blood*, l. 10.
  (b) /æ/ and /ɑ:/ are distributed as in RP (WL 21–6; see p. 28). /æ/ is realized as [ɛ̞], or as a diphthong, [ɛi] (figure 4.4; WL 21; *bag*, l. 35).
  (c) Unlike RP, the final vowel of *city* etc. is /i/ and not /ɪ/ (WL 19, 20).
2 /h/ is almost invariably absent. When it is present, it is likely to be in a stressed position (*happened*, l. 26).
3 The glottal stop, [ʔ], is extremely common in Cockney speech. As well as in the environments in which it occurs in RP, it is also found:
  (a) accompanying /p/ between vowels (*paper*, l. 2)
  (b) representing /t/ between vowels and before pause (WL 1–6 etc; *butterfly*, l. 18; *wet*, l. 3).
4 (a) The contrast between /θ/ and /f/ is variably lost:

initially	*thin*	/fɪn/
medially	*Cathy*	/kæfi:/
finally	*both*	/bouf/

  (b) Similarly, the contrast between /ð/ and /v/ is also often lost:

medially	*together*	/təgɛvə/, l. 20)
and finally	*bathe*	/beiv/

  Initially, /d/ or zero is more likely to be heard for /ð/
  e.g. *the* (l. 4) is /də/
    they (l. 11) is /ei/

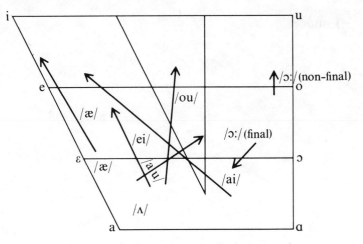

Figure 4.4 Typical realizations of certain Cockney vowels

5 (a) When /ɔ:/ is final it is realized much as the vowel of *pore* in some
    RP speech; when /ɔ:/ is non-final, its realization is much closer,
    [o:] (figure 4.4; cf. WL 45, 48).
   (b) As a result of this difference, there is a distinction made in the
    speech of London and of areas to the south of the city, which is
    absent in RP, between pairs of words like:

    paws [pɔəz] and   *pause* [po:z] (WL 48, 49)
    bored [bɔəd] and   *board* [bo:d]

The distinction is made on the basis of the presence or absence of
inflection. Where, for example, plural, third person singular, or
genitive *s* is added to a word-final /ɔ:/, [ɔə] is still found, rather than
[o:].

6 (a) When /l/ occurs finally after a vowel e.g. *Paul* (WL 30), *well* (l.
    18); before a consonant in the same syllable e.g. *milk*; or as a
    syllable in itself e.g. *table*, it is realized as a vowel. Thus: [poʊ,
    wɛʊ, mɪʊk, tæɪbʊ]. When the preceding vowel is /ɔ:/, there may
    be complete loss of /l/. Thus *Pauls* may be [po:z], i.e. identical
    with *pause*.
    These comments on /l/ are true not only for London but also for
    the Home Counties i.e. those counties adjoining London, and it
    is a feature which seems to be spreading.
   (b) The vowels which represent /l/ can alter the quality of the vowels
    preceding them in such a way as to make homonyms of pairs like:

    pool   *pull* (WL 28, 29)
    doll   *dole* (cf. *doll, pole*, WL 31, 29)
    peal   *pill*

This tendency appears to be spreading too.

7 Certain diphthongs are markedly different from RP in their realization (see figure 4.4).
   (a) /ei/ is [æɪ] (WL 40; *paper*, l. 2)
   (b) /ou/ is [æʉ] (WL 12; *soaked*, l. 9)
   (c) /ai/ is [ɑɪ] (WL 9; *inside*, l. 3)
   (d) /au/ may be [æə] (*surrounded*, l. 51) and may produce an intrusive /r/ (see pp. 31-32) as *now*, l. 54.
8 –*ing* is /ɪn/
   (a) *laying*, l. 1) (see p. 34)
   (b) In *nothing*, *something* etc. –*ing* may be [ɪŋk] (*anything*, l. 5)
9 When they are initial, /p, t, k/ are heavily aspirated, more so than in RP. In the case of /t/, there is affrication (the tongue leaves the alveolar ridge slowly and [s] is produced before the vowel begins). Thus *tea*, l. 5, is [tsi:].

The recording

The speaker is a working man of about fifty who has lived all his life in London. His accent is quite strong, though certain features, such as the use of /f/ for /θ/, are not so obvious. He is talking about his time in hospital just before his release after an operation.

The reader of the word list is younger and her accent is not as strong. Notice the variability in the realization of final /t/, which is sometimes [ʔ] and sometimes [t].

I came back to the bed, like, after breakfast . . . I was just like laying on it a bit and reading th . : . the paper, and, I don't know, I thought to myself, I don't know, I feel wet in my pyjamas and I looked inside . . . and put my hand in it . . . it is wet wh . . . how . . . how the dickens . . . I
5 ain't spilt any tea or anything down there. So I thought to myself, I know, I'll go out in the ablution place, like, there . . . they've got some little radiators . . . all little individual places . . . got a little radiator there . . . put my pyjamas on to dry, I just thought it was some water . . . of course when I got out there the dressing that was on me, that was soaked in a
10 . . . yeh, like a . . . a watery blood . . . so, course I went and saw the sister and er . . . they put another dressing on it . . . they put another dressing on it . . . yeh . . . yeh . . . it wasn't . . . wasn't long before that was soaked and all, Fred . . . wasn't long before that was soaked . . . so of course I went and had another one done . . . so I said to the . . . the nurse, I said—
15 guess to what it was—it was like where they . . . they'd taken the tubes out, and I said to her have they opened up? She said no, there's nothing, like o . . . a . . . actually open . . . it's seeping . . . it was seeping through it, yeh. Well . . . I said, well, I said, if you put s . . . some, like, little butterfly stitches over that first of all . . . out of . . . er . . . er . . . plaster like . . . you
20 know . . . hold that together. I said well then . . . put a dressing and a big

plaster on it, so she done that, but it still didn't . . . yeh . . . it still seeped
through . . . and course I begin to get worried, and when . . . when she
done it, like, the third time . . . took it off—I'm laying there—I could see
it, it was running away from me like tears. Yeh . . . but yeh, but anyway
25 . . . yeh . . . yeh . . . that's what I say . . . and of course, what . . . what had
happened, also, that was the Saturday, wasn't it?, yeh, I . . . er . . . had
my pyjamas . . . I . . . I'd just changed my pyjamas so I said to Rene, I
phoned Rene there, and I said, could you bring me another one of my
old pairs of pyjamas, I said, cos, I said, some stain had come through it,
30 you know, how, you know . . . round the waistband and that. So she
brought me in a new pair of 'jamas in the afternoon and I went and
changed them and . . . and that . . . but, blimey, before she went home,
they were worse than the other pair, weren't they? It'd come through and
it had soaked right through and down the leg, and the other pair had
35 dried off a bit in the bag so I thought, well, I'll have to keep them, so . . . I
did get it done again and er . . . I changed into pyjamas . . . well of course
when it come to the Sunday, I'm going home Sunday, made
arrangements for . . . she's going to pick me up about ten . . . so of course
I had to see the . . . the sister . . . and er . . . she said I'd like the doctor to
40 see that . . . well . . . time's going on, so I phoned Rene in the morning
and said don't pick me up at ten, make it nearer twelve, sort of thing . . .
it'd give me a chance . . . and er . . . anyway . . . it was a long while before
this doctor come up. It was only, like, the young one, see, weekend one.
But anyway, the sister, she was getting a bit worried. She said he don't
45 seem to be coming, so she had a look, and she said, well if it was my
decision she wouldn't let me home . . . and er . . . anyhow I more or less
pleaded with her, I said well they're coming here in a little while, I said, if
you'd've told me before, I said, I would have made arrangements and
cancelled it . . . anyway . . . she was still worried so she went and she
50 found this young doctor. He come along . . . still laying there, you know,
on my bed, sort of thing, surrounded. Eventually he comes ten to twelve
. . . and he has a look and . . . he's, like, with the nurse there, he wasn't
with the sister, but anyway he said, well, he said, you don't seem to be
weeping now . . . he said, I don't think it'll weep any more, he said . . .
55 erm . . . he said, well, if I let you go home, he said, he said, they'll have to
be dressed twice a day . . . he said, and he said . . . twice a day, he said,
while it's . . . comes away a bit wet, he said, and once a day, he said, when
it's dry, sort of thing.

Notes

1   The past tense of COME is variably *came* e.g. l. 1 and *come* e.g. l. 37,
     43, 50 (see p. 15).
2   The past tense of the full verb DO is *done* (l. 21, 23; see p. 15).

3 First person singular, negative, of the auxiliary *have* is *ain't* (l. 5; see p. 14).

4 Third person singular, negative, of the auxiliary *do* is *don't* (l. 44; see p. 17).

5 The use of *lay* for standard English *lie* (l. 1) is not restricted to any region, and standard English speakers often seem to have to concentrate hard to produce the appropriate form!

6 Items like *and all* (meaning, *as well*) (l. 13), *like* (throughout), *and that* (1.32), are also not restricted to any particular region, and are best regarded simply as features of colloquial speech.

7 Exclamations like *how the dickens* (l. 4) and *blimey* (l. 32) are colloquial, found in a number of regions of Britain, and probably used more by older people.

8 *cos* (l. 29) represents /kɒz/, a colloquial form of *because*.

II Norwich

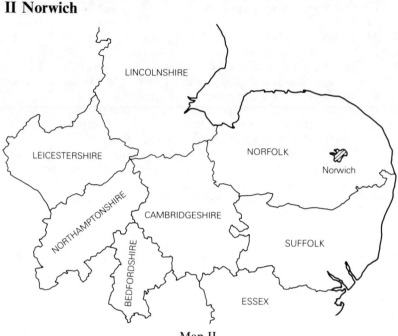

Map II

1   The speech of Norwich in particular, and East Anglia in general, is southern.
   (a) /ʊ/ and /ʌ/ are both present (WL 4, 5)
   (b) /æ/ and /ɑ:/ are distributed as in RP (WL 21–6)
   (c) the final vowel of *city* etc. is /i/, not /ɪ/ as in RP (WL 19, 20; see p. 30).
   But it differs from the accents of London and the Home Counties (see p. 40) in that /l/ in *milk, pull, bottle* etc. is not realized as a vowel. Rather, like RP, there is a 'dark' /l/, [ɫ], with the back of the tongue raised towards the soft palate (WL 27–31).
2   In Norfolk and neighbouring areas (see p. 35) /j/ is variably lost after all consonants. (*humorous*, l. 1; *during*, l. 44).
3   An older English distinction, lost in RP, is maintained. Thus RP homonyms are quite distinct in Norwich.

/u:/	/ɔu/	
moan	*mown*	
sole	*soul*	
nose	*knows*	(WL 38,39)

4   For some speakers, words like *moon* and *boot* have the same vowel (/u:/) as *moan* and *boat*, such pairs being homonyms (WL 11, 12).

5   The RP distinction between /ɪə/ and /ɛə/ is not present, and so, for example, both *beer* and *bear* are pronounced /bɛ:/ (WL 14, 15; *hear*, l. 21; *here*, l. 18).

6   While /h/ has been preserved in rural East Anglia, it has been partly lost in Norwich. Thus in the recording it is generally present in stressed words e.g. *humorous* (l. 1) and *husband* (l. 4), but sometimes missing in unstressed words. Note (l. 28) that, within a second, *he* is produced first with /h/ and then without.

7   Certain words which have /ou/ in RP may have /ʊ/, e.g. *home* (l. 29) and *suppose* (l. 41).

8   Words like *room* and *broom*, and (as in other eastern accents—see p. 28) *roof* and *hoof*, have /ʊ/ rather than /u:/.

9   Stressed vowels are long, while unstressed vowels are much reduced, giving a distinctive rhythm to East Anglian speech. Associated with the reduction of unstressed vowels is the loss of consonants e.g. the loss of /v/ in *side of it* (l. 17).

10   *off* is /ɔ:f/ (l. 25).

11   The glottal stop [ʔ] variably represents /t/ between vowels, and also accompanies /p/, /t/, /k/, particularly between vowels e.g. *bottom* (l. 20), *dirty* (l. 25), *city* (WL 19).

12   *–ing* is /ən/.

The recording

The speaker is a woman about fifty years old who has lived in Norwich all her life. Her accent is quite strong. She recalls how she first met her husband.

The reader of the word list is a younger woman with not so strong an accent.

I've got something humorous happened to me, one thing I'll never forget.

—What's that?

Eh? We . . . well th . . . this is, this is when I first met my husband . . .
5 cos I generally . . . you know, my daughter always laugh about that, we went and had a drink . . . erm . . . one night. I don't know if you know the Blue Room? near the erm . . . do you know the . . . erm . . . Yeh.

Well we went in there one night to have a drink. There was erm . . . two girl friends and me . . . this was before I married, see and, well this
10 was the night, see, when I met my husband and erm you know they was like b . . . the fellows was buying us drinks and that, see, and er my friend and her sister, oh, she say, we don't want to go with them, she said, let's give them the slip . . . right . . . well we ran up er Prince of Wales Road and opposite the, well, that's . . . that was the Regent then, that's the
15 ABC now, there's a fruiterers, Empire Fruit Stores, I don't know if it's

still there, is it? Well there was this here fruits . . . er . . . fruitstore and
that and they had a passage way at the side of it, see. Well my friends said
to me, oh, they said, Flo we'll get in here and give them the slip . . . I went
to go in first . . . thought that was a long passage and that wasn't . . . they
20 had forty steps and I fell right to the bottom . . . yeh . . . and there was
me, see, and we . . . and we could hear . . . y'know they could hear these
here fellows come run . . . running up behind, see, so my friends said, oh
quick, Flo have fell down a lot of stairs. Well the one what's my
husband, he said, let her lay there, he said. We've been treating you all
25 night, they said, and you do us the dirty and run off . . . and they let me
lay there. Well, any rate my friends, I managed to stumble up. I had two
big bumps on my head . . . I had a black eye . . . and course erm the . . .
erm . . . see . . . my husband to be then erm he well he let me lay there well
when I got home, see, my father said to me, the first thing . . . whatever
30 have you done? I said, I got knocked down by a bike . . . that was the first
thing that come into my head . . . yeh and I . . . I gen . . . generally tell my
daughter about that. I said . . . she say, that's what you get, Mum, she
say, for making a fellow, she said letting a fellow, she said, buy you the
drink and then, she said, running away from him. I say yeh, but that, you
35 know, that's sort of like . . . well then he come round the next night to see
how I was and that's how we got acquainted. He said, that'll teach you
. . . he said, er yeh, he said, that'll teach you, he say . . . taking drinks off
anyone he said and try, he said, you thought, he said, you were going to
slip off, he said . . . erm . . . he said, did you know there was any steps?
40 and I said, no I didn't . . . I thought that was a long passage, see, and
there was just, there was forty steps that go right down I suppose to . . .
and lead into a door at the back of this here fruit shop.

Yeh, well I lived, erm, see, when I got married, see my husband was in
the RAF during the war and then, erm, my mother died, well, like when I
45 was young . . . so my . . . I kept house /fəm/ . . . for my Dad, and lived
there see . . . see cos my husband was a . . . abroad well he was abroad
then in the RAF . . . see, and then he got er killed, see, one morning when
he was going to work, see . . . and I . . . and we've now been up here erm
well it's five years last June.

Notes

1   The third person singular, present tense is not marked by /s/.
    Thus: *laugh* (l. 5), *say* (l. 33, 34, 37; see p. 16).
2   The absence of /s/ applies also to auxiliary *have* (l. 23).
3   Introduction of a relative clause by *what* (l. 23; see p. 17).
4   *lay* (l. 26): standard English *lie* (as in the London recording).
5   *that* is used where standard English would have *it* (l. 40).
6   Note intrusive /r/ in *by a bike* [ʙəɹəbaɪk̚ʔ] (l. 30; see p. 31).

III Bristol

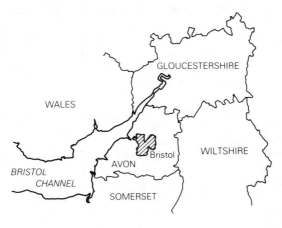

Map III

1 The speech of Bristol, and the southwest generally, makes a distinction between pairs like *put* and *putt* (WL 4, 5). The vowel of *putt*, however, is [ə], and it seems that, unlike in RP, there are not two distinct phonemes /ə/ and /ʌ/ (see p. 28).

2 There is no /æ/–/ɑː/ contrast (WL 21–26), and /æ/ is realized as [a] (figure 4.5 and map 2).

3 (a) There is post-vocalic /r/ (see p. 31 and map 3). /r/ is quite retroflex in quality, that is, with the tip of the tongue bending backwards towards the hard palate (WL 14–18, 34–7, 42–4; note contrast with 45). Note that the equivalents to the RP diphthongs /ɪə/, /ɛə/, and /ʊə/ are /ɪr/ (WL 14), /ɛr/ (WL 15), and /ur/ (WL 42).

(b) A feature of speech known as 'Bristol l', which is confined to the immediate area of Bristol, is the presence of /l/ following word final /ə/. Thus *America* may be /əmɛrɪkəl/ and *Eva* /iːvəl/. In such cases *Eva* and *evil* are homophones. Bristol l is not so common, generally stigmatized, and cannot be heard on our recording (see p. 32).

(c) Notice that dark /l/ (see p. 44) is very dark, that is, the raising of the back of the tongue to soft palate is most marked.

4 There is a tendency, though probably less common than in London, for the contrast between /θ/ and /f/ to be lost, but again there is no example of this on our recording.

5 The glottal stop [ʔ] may represent /t/ before pause e.g. *Pete*, [piːʔ] (l. 17) (but note that in l. 13, *Pete* is [piːt])

6   The diphthongs /ei/ and /ou/ are rather wide, [ɛɪ] and [ɔu] (figure 4.5 and WL 8, 40, 41, and 29, 38, 39).

7   *–ing* is /ɪn/.

8   As in London speech, in words like *anything, something –ing* may be /ɪŋk/ (l. 3, *something*).

9   (a) By comparison with RP, short vowels are often of longer duration. Thus: *job* [jɑ·b] (l. 49), *mad* [ma·d] (l. 11), and *bucket* [bə·kɪ·ʔ] (l. 58).

   (b) In certain words there is a stronger vowel than its equivalent in RP e.g. /gʊdnɛs/ (l. 34) as opposed to /gʊdnəs/, or /gʊdnɪs/ in RP.

   (c) Similarly, a vowel followed by a consonant is found where in RP there is a syllabic consonant e.g. ['bəʔən] as opposed to [bʌtn̩] *button*.

10 /h/ is variably absent. Thus, (l. 3), it is present four times in succession (*He'd had his fixed, he said*), but is absent on the next occasion (l. 4), where *had* is [ad].

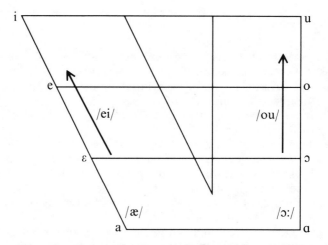

Figure 4.5 Typical realizations of certain vowels in Bristol speech

The recording

The speaker is a housewife, about thirty years old. Though she quite clearly comes from the Bristol area, her accent is less broad than most on the tape. As mentioned above, local features of pronunciation seem to become more frequent when she becomes excited.

   You know . . . our overflow . . . well it does overf . . . well a fortnight 'ago, next door neighbour said to us—mind, his overflows every day—

erm . . . could Pete do something about it. He'd had his fixed, he said. So
Pete came in and went up and had a look it's it's the . . . erm . . . you
5   know, the immersion heater system. I think it's where the ball thing
doesn't close up properly, so the water drips out the overflow. Well that
was fair enough. Pete came up and had a go at it and ever since then two
days apart from yesterday it's the only time ours has dripped out at all.
Every day of the week theirs's dripped out. So yesterday afternoon Pete
10 comes home from fishing. I'm sure he waited for Pete, because he knows
Pete won't say anything, see, cos I was mad . . . and er Pete comes in, and
I heard all these doors going and I went out and the hot water tap was on
so I said: Who's turned the hot water tap on? Pete said: He's just asked
me again, can I do something about our overflow because it was pouring
15 out yesterday; something had gone really wrong yesterday, the thing
wasn't working at all. So I said: Well you did tell him that his hasn't
stopped since he said. No, says Pete. He's moaning about ours
overflowing. Mine overflows into the bunker, mind, my bunker, and
flows out. And this morning I come down, and blow me if this isn't isn't
20 overflowing again, this one. I was mad. When Pete went I couldn't even
watch the film I was watching. I was so mad, I thought, well the least Pete
could have done was said: Well, look, you know fair enough, I agree,
mine is overflowing but so's yours. I mean, would you have the cheek to
tell a neighbour to mend something when your own wasn't fixed . . . well
25 it's our water that's making his wall damp. Not his own water, mind,
that flows out every day of the week. Just mine that's done three times in
a fortnight. I was mad, Jill, really mad . . . oh, no, that was the guttering
that . . . and that was his fault as well . . . no no no ne . . . no cos tha . . . it
runs from ours down next door and down again to their drain. No, it was
30 his cos he's never cleaned his gutters out. Us, thinking we were being
good cleaned ours out regularly, but all we really did, see, it built up, the
water then stayed in ours because it didn't go over the top of the dirt.
Yeh. That is fixed now, though, since Pete got up there, that's been
perfectly all right, even with the heavy weather, thank goodness. Do
35 have these problems, don't we, with these silly things . . . I mean the
point is, really, it's quite a simple job to fix it. Pete's Dad said really all
you need is a new washer, but, I don't know where your . . . erm . . .
immersion, you know, your tank is but ours is high in the airing
cupboard. The shelf that's in the airing cupboard won't support the
40 weight of anybody, and from outside you can't get your head up and
over the top. Well . . . no no, and it means that Pete's got to s . . . kind of
get up and over, well, what's worrying me is, you've got to turn the water
off, well that's fair enough but my fire heats the water, well if he can just
take the arm off, replace the washer and put it back, that's good, but if
45 anything goes wrong I've then got to let the fire out, because I can't have
the fire going if the water can't be replaced and so what is really a simple
job, knowing us, could take all day. So I'd rather it dripped out there a

bit longer ... nothing. He reckoned he had somebody in, but, I mean, if I
had somebody in I would expect the job done properly, I mean, fair
50   enough, Pete's just bent our arm, well, his dad said that won't last long
because, you know, a couple of weeks and the arm'll naturally put itself
back up. He said it's the new washer, but course it was doing a new
washer down at the church that Pete's dad chopped all his hand the
other week and had to have a week off work. And it's thinking of things
55   like that that can happen to people who don't usually have calamities
that makes me a bit worried about letting Pete do ours ... oh well I ... I
expect so. It was this morning I went out this morning to fill my coal
bucket, it wa ... well I don't I don't feel I should complain, because mine
does drip out now and then, but knowing his does it every day ... I mean
60   it's a bit off in't it Jill ... anyway ... but I will get ours fixed in due
course, ... but when I'm sure it isn't going to cause a calamity at the same
time.

Notes

1   Notice the infrequency of fillers like *kind of*, and *like*.
2   *drips out the overflow* (l. 6) cf. standard English, *out of the overflow*
(see p. 19).
3   *course* (l. 52) = *of course*.

IV South Wales (Pontypridd)

Map IV

1   In south Wales the distribution of /æ/ and /ɑ:/ is generally as in the north of England (see p. 28 and map 2). The contrast between the vowels, however, is usually one of length only. Thus *cat* [kat] and *cart* [ka:t] (WL 21, 26).

2   (a) There is no post-vocalic /r/, except in the speech of some native speakers of Welsh (map 3).

    (b) /r/ is normally a tap [ɾ], that is, the tip of the tongue makes a rapid tap against the alveolar ridge (as in the speech of some RP speakers in the pronunciation of words like *very* and *marry* (e.g. *tramline, right,* l. 2).

3   As in Bristol, there is not a /ʌ/–/ə/ contrast. Words like *putt* (WL 5) have /ə/, contrasting with /ʊ/ in *put* (WL 4).

4   Words like *city* and *seedy* have /iː/ as the final vowel (WL 19, 20).

5   /l/ is not 'dark' (see p. 44) in any environment (WL 27–31).

6   In words like *tune, few, used,* we find /ɪu/ rather than /juː/ (*used,* l. 2). This diphthong is preserved even after /r/ and /l/. Thus most speakers make a distinction between pairs such as *blew* /blɪu/ and *blue* /bluː/, *threw* and *through*. *Blew* and *blue* are contrasted in the short exchange at the end of the word list (see p. 52 and figure 4.6).

7   Between vowels, when the first vowel is stressed, consonants may be doubled. So *city* (WL 19) is [sˈɪtiː].

8   /h/ is usually absent, but may be present in stressed positions e.g. *him,* l. 25.

9   (a) /ei/ is narrow and may even be a monophthong [e·] (figure 4.6 WL 8, 40, 41).

(b) In certain areas of south Wales a distinction is made between pairs of words like *daze* /deiz/ and *days* /dɛɪz/. /ɛɪ/ occurs where there is *i* or *y* in the spelling. The speakers on the tape do not make this distinction.

10   /ou/ is narrow and may even be a monophthong [o:] (WL 12, 29, 38, 39). This tendency may result in such pairs as *so* and *soar* being homonyms.

11   The vowel /ɜ:/, as in *bird* (WL 16), is produced with the lips rounded, approaching [ø:].

12   Intonation in Welsh English is very much influenced by the Welsh language. Though quite noticeable in the recording, it is less striking than in the speech of many Welshmen, including those whose first language is English. Welsh is learned as a first language normally only in the west and north west of the country.

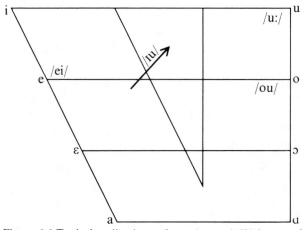

Figure 4.6 Typical realizations of certain south Wales vowels

The recording

The speaker is a young man from Pontypridd, whose accent, though quite obviously Welsh, is not particularly strong. He is talking about an accident that happened to someone as a child.

The word list reader is a young woman from Neath. Again, although she is clearly Welsh, her accent is not very strong.

At the end of the word list there is the following exchange to demonstrate the difference between *blew* and *blue*:

What did the wind do yesterday?
Erm . . . the wind blew /blɪu/ strongly.
All right . . . and what colour are your jeans?
My jeans are blue /blu:/.

The tramlines . . . ah, they used to have . . . erm . . . from the pit there used to be a tramline right to the top of the mountain . . . used to work on a . . . a pulley sort of system, I should think, I was too young to know then. They used to have about fifteen to twenty big pit drums on this wire
5 rope, and I would say it must have stretched, bottom to top, about three and a half, maybe four miles, and of course we'd winch up on it, pulled up, cos all the kids would be running up, jumping on . . . and, er, I would say, well there was one boy, how old is Gevin . . . must be about thirty-eight he's . . . jumped on and he fell off and it cut his leg clean off. But
10 they're big metal drums, they weighed well, they must weigh about a ton with nothing in them, so you can imagine when they're full . . . and of course when they come down the journey again . . . they're coming down at a fair speed cos they let them go down quite a bit and then they got them . . . on automatic brake, I think, and it slows them down . . . we
15 used to come down there. We used to jump on them on the top and ride down . . . things you do when you're young . . .

About ten, twelve . . . he won't . . . he's got a false leg but he won't wear it. When he wears it, you know . . . when he first had it he used to
20 wear it . . . and er, he was quite a big boy, as all Welshmen are, they're all broad, but he must be up to . . . something like . . . twenty-eight stone and he's really fat, it just hangs off him. He sits and watches television and he has two pound of apples and er say a pound of chocolate . . . and . . . his mother makes sandwiches, she makes a loaf of bread . . . just for
25 him, for sandwiches, as a snack . . . well most of the boys who drink with him in the club . . . erm . . . were with Gevin when he done it . . . when he done it . . . they used all used to ride up on the . . . the journey, aye I should think every boy in Cil has done it.

——You did it, did you?
30 Oh, aye, regular.

We'd always be warned—don't ride on the drums . . . (Welsh) . . . straight down the bottom and wait for them to come up and you'd you'd run up along side them and just jump on . . . the most dangerous thing about that was . . . er . . . was the rope, the metal rope, which was about
35 two inches in diameter, and it used to whip. And of course you imagine a steel rope whipping . . . well it'd cut a man clean in half . . . you never see the dangers when you're young, do you?

Notes

1 *Two pound of apples* (l. 23) see p. 19.
2 *Done* as past tense of DO (l. 27) see p. 15.
3 *Aye = yes* (l. 30): common in the north of England, Scotland, Ireland and Wales.

V West Midlands

Wolverhampton
Walsall
West Bromwich •
BIRMINGHAM
Coventry

Map V

This is the accent spoken in Birmingham, Wolverhampton, and a number of other towns in that area (see map).

1   The accent of the West Midlands is northern in that:
   (a) /æ/ is found in words such as *dance*, *daft* etc. (see p. 28; WL 21–6).
   (b) Pairs of words like *put* and *putt* are not distinct, /ʊ/ being the vowel in both (see p. 27; WL 4, 5).

2   The accent nevertheless has certain southern characteristics.
   (a) The final vowel of *city* and *seedy* etc. is /iː/ (see p. 30; WL 19, 20; cf. Liverpool).
   (b) The diphthongs /ei/ and /ou/ are wide, being realized as [æɪ] and [ʌʊ] (figure 4.7; WL 8, 40, 41 and 12, 29, 38, 39).

3   /iː/ is [ɜi] (figure 4.7; WL 14, 19, 20).
   /uː/ is [ɜu] (figure 4.7; WL 28).

4   /ai/ is [ɔi] (figure 4.7; WL 9, 46, 47).

5   /ɪ/ is very close, [i] (figure 4.7; WL 1, 19).

6   /ɜː/ and /ɛə/ are merged as [œː] e.g. *bear* and *bird* on the word list. The influence of RP is, however, discernible in the attempted distinction on the word list between *fur* and *fair*. This merger is not found throughout the West Midlands (figure 4.7).

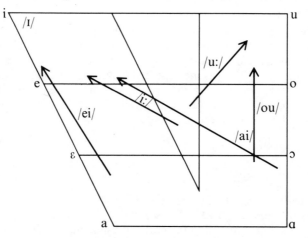

Figure 4.7 Typical realizations of certain West Midlands vowels

7 /h/ is usually absent.
8 *–ing* is /ɪn/.
9 Note *one* is /wɒn/ but *won* is /wʊn/ (l. 24; see p. 27).
10 There are few glottal stops.

The recording

The speaker, who is a caretaker, is from Walsall and has a very distinctive West Midlands accent. After saying something about his evening habits, he goes on to talk about his footballing days and then about the problems of Walsall Football Club.

I don't go out much, not in the week, you know. I go out one night a week, and if the wife isn't bothered. I won't, you know, I don't bother. Well, the wife and the daughter generally go out together and I stop in, you know, with the lad . . . but er as g . . . the wife and the daughter
5 they've booked up a show what the women have got up or something, eight fifty to see that man who works . . . impersonates a woman . . . what's his name him who impersonates the women on the television . . .
  The other night I couldn't get in . . . interested in it about ho . . . homosexuals, you know, and I said to my wife, I says, er, are you coming
10 to bed? Her says, no, I'm going to see the finish of this. I says, all right then, goodnight, and I went up to bed. I mean . . . I'm not, you know, like that . . .
  I used to be keen. I used to be a good footballer myself . . . yeh . . .
  Goodyears and all those, you know, they was high class teams, I mean
15 you played for the honour then, I mean, you didn't get nothing out of it . . .
  No, no, well, er me and the captain of Guest Keens, we had a trial for Walsall and er we came up the one week and they says, come the next week and play again, see, well in the meantime we've got an important
20 match for the works team, cup final, and the captain says, are you going to Walsall? I said no, the works team's more important to me, see. Course we didn't go, and we had a nasty post card off Walsall FC about it, cos we didn't turn up . . .
  Well I won the one cup for them really in . . . erm . . . 1948 . . . er we
25 was er winning one-none half-time, and the second half I got three goals, and we won four . . . a . . . an theys . . . and they made me go and have the cup, cos, they said, you've won this cup and you're going to have it, and I . . . I . . . present . . . presented with it, you know . . .
  I could have done, yes, If I'd have stuck to it, you know, but . . . er . . .
30 well . . . when, you know . . . no, no . . . but, I mean, you didn't get a lot then if you played professional, I mean, it was a poor wage then, years ago . . . but it . . . it was an honour to play, they didn't play for the money like they do today . . . well, they've got to make it while they're fit, cos you never know what's going to happen . . .

35 Well Dave Mackay was on the wireless this morning before I come
out, you know, and they was interviewing him, the reporter, and he said
he . . . he couldn't understand it why they couldn't score at home . . . I
mean, but win away, you know . . .
        . . . played for Derby, half-back, didn't he? Yes, I do. I always like to see
40 them win, and that, but er . . . something . . . lacking there, definitely . . .
    Well Walsall can if they dish the football up. Course they couldn't
keep me away years ago. I used to go to every . . . well, I think it's been
about six or eight years, when they played Sunderland down here in the
cup, and Liverpool . . . I paid a man to do my job, here of a Saturday
45 afternoon to go and see the two matches. And when I come back . . . I
was away, say, two hours . . . I'd still got the same work to do . . .
nothing had been done . . .   .
    Well er they never spent no money but they got local talent . . . they
got a lot of local talent what come up . . . you know, like . . . out of the
50 amateur sides. That's where they go wrong, they don't go to the proper
matches . . . er . . . like Shrewsbury, now, Chick Bates, they had him
from Stourbridge for about two hundred and fifty pound fee . . . and
he's scoring two or three goals a match now . . . I mean, Walsall could've
done with a man like him.

Notes
1   There are examples of multiple negation (see p. 13):
        You didn't get nothing out of it (l. 15);
        Well they never spent no money (l. 48).
2   Past tense of COME is *come* (l. 35, 45, 49).
3   (a) *I says* (l. 10) is 'present historic' (see p. 17).
    (b) *was* is the past tense form of BE, not only for the third person
        singular:
        We was winning (l. 25)
        they was interviewing him (l. 36).
4   *What* introduces a relative clause (see p. 17):
        they got a lot of local talent what come up (l. 49).
5   *something* (l. 5) is /sʊmət/.
6   (a) *not bothered* (l. 2) = not keen.
    (b) *the lad* (l. 4) i.e. his son cf. *the wife*.
    (c) *FC* (l. 22) = Football Club.
    (d) *wireless* (l. 35) is not regional but old-fashioned. It bears the same
        relationship to *radio* as *gramophone* does to *record player* (see p.
        9).
7   *postcard off Walsall FC* (l. 22) = standard English: *from Walsall FC*
    (see p. 19).
8   *you* is /jau/.
9   Dave Mackay (l. 35) is a former Scottish international footballer,
    now the manager of Walsall.
10 *her* (l. 10) = *she*.
11 The definite article before a vowel is ð e.g. *th amateur* (l. 49).

VI Bradford

NORTH YORKSHIRE

LANCASHIRE
Bradford — Leeds
WEST YORKSHIRE
Huddersfield

SOUTH YORKSHIRE
Sheffield

Map VI

1 The accent of Bradford, and of Yorkshire generally, is northern in that:
   (a) Words like *dance* and *daft* have /æ/ (WL 22, 23; see p. 28). For some Yorkshire speakers, /æ/ and /ɑ:/ are differentiated only by length. For them the vowels are [a] and [a:] (figure 4.8), *Pam* and *palm* being [pam] and [pa:m]. This is not the case for the speakers on the tape, for whom /ɑ:/ is a little further back.
   (b) There is no distinction between pairs of words like *put* and *putt*, both having /ʊ/ (WL 4, 5; see p. 27).
   (c) The final vowel in words like *city* and *seedy* is /ɪ/ (WL 19, 20; see p. 30).
2 (a) i /ei/ is either a narrow diphthong or a monophthong, [e:] (e.g. *plate*, WL 40; *mate*, WL 52; figure 4.8).
       ii But for some speakers, words which have *eigh* in the spelling (e.g. *weight*, WL 41) have /ɛi/ (figure 4.8).
   (b) i /ou/ is also a narrow diphthong or a monophthong, [o̞:] (e.g. *boat*, WL 12; *nose*, WL 38; figure 4.8).
       ii But, for some speakers, many words which have *ow* or *ou* in the spelling (e.g. *knows*, WL 39) have /ɔu/ (figure 4.8). Thus for these speakers *nose* and *knows* are not homonyms. This distinction (also made in Norwich—see p. 44) is being lost, younger speakers generally using /ou/ for both sets of words.

3   Pairs of words like *pore* (which has *r* in the spelling) and *paw* (WL
    44, 45) are distinguished. Words without *r* have /ɔ:/ ([ǫ:]); words
    with *r* have /ɔə/ ([ǫə]) (figure 4.8). This distinction is also made by
    some RP speakers.
4   (a) /ɛ/ is [ɛ̞] i.e. more open than in southern accents (WL 2; figure
        4.8).
    (b) /u:/ is [u:] as compared with the more central realization of this
        vowel in Lancashire (WL 28; figure 4.8).
    (c) /ai/ is /aɛ/ (WL 46; figure 4.8).
5   In the West Riding (which includes Bradford) and other areas of
    Yorkshire, /b, d, g/ become /p, t, k/ when they immediately precede
    a voiceless consonant (i.e. a consonant produced without vibration
    of the vocal chords). Thus *Bradford* is /brætfəd/ and *could swing* (l.
    32) is /kʊtswɪŋ/.
6   /r/ is a tap (see p. 51).
7   /t/ when final may be realized as a glottal stop [ʔ] (e.g. *that* l. 40; see
    p. 34).
8   *–ing* is /ɪn/.
9   /h/ is generally absent.
10 *make* and *take* are /mɛk/ and /tɛk/ (l. 20).

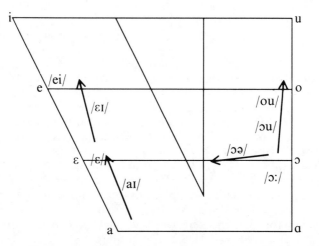

Figure 4.8 Typical realizations of certain Bradford vowels

The recording

The speaker is a man who has lived in Bradford all his life. His accent is
quite marked, but notice the variable presence of /h/. He talks about his
schooldays and events in his youth.

——Did you ever have any teacher you were scared of or . . . you know, you couldn't stand?

Oh, yes, definitely . . . oh, aye . . . a Miss Ingham . . . and Mr Priestley, I was rather scared of him . . . you know, but . . . Miss Ingham, when I
5 was a kid, she . . . she always . . . to me she seemed rather vicious, you know . . . er . . . instead of . . . you know, she'd knee you with her knee as she came round, you know, you were sat on the chair . . . and she'd kick her knee into your back if she thought . . . you know . . . and she was rather vicious, I used to think . . . thin lipped . . . rather . . . oh, aye . . .
10 used to frighten you . . . Priestley was . . . he was all right w . . . I . . . I think I was scared of him, really scared, you know, and when he came in . . . aah! I couldn't think . . . I couldn't . . . he looked over the door sometimes . . . you know . . . oh, deary me, over the glass partition, you know, in the door . . . oh, he's coming in . . . and, honestly, I couldn't
15 think when he were in sometimes . . . especially if he took us in mental arithmetic . . . oo, help . . . and when he took us in ear tests, that were as bad, nearly . . . he'd tell you . . . he'd say sometimes, put two fingers in your mouth . . . and, you know, he'd have you putting two fingers in . . . three . . . four . . . five . . . put your foot in . . . aye, you know, that sort of
20 thing he'd make you open your mouth that way . . . I mean, you couldn't sing with your teeth, he said, like that, you know . . . you've got to open your mouth to sing . . . and he used to open his . . . and he'd about two teeth in the middle . . . sort of thing, you know, all of us kids, you know, looked and he seemed to have three or four, you know, missing or more
25 happen just two good . . . oh aye, he were a lad, I tell you . . . certainly f . . . fri . . . well, I won't say, frightened you, but you were frightened of him, you know . . . he . . . he . . . er . . . oh dear . . . as I say, he used to put such a fear into me I couldn't think . . . I remember that quite well . . . aye . . . oh wasn't I glad when he went out . . .
30 Well one of the funniest ever . . . was when we were . . . playing on a swing bridge, you know . . . and er . . . you were seeing how far you could swing the bridge out . . . and then . . . it wasn't funny really . . . the . . . but, you mean we laughed afterwards about it . . . on the canal . . . it was swing . . . at t'swing bridge at Seven Arches . . . swinging it out, you
35 know, and you jump and see how far you can go on it . . . and then one of them jumped into the canal, you see . . . you see . . . but that didn't finish . . . you see we were . . . thought of making . . . er . . . dry his clothes . . . so they made a fire . . . took his clothes off, you see and . . . they couldn't get any . . . slow burning stuff, it were all quick burning stuff, you see . . .
40 and there they were running round with bracken and things like that, making a big fire, and one kid . . . holding his shirt, you see, up to t'fire, and it caught fire . . . burnt his shirt . . . wasn't funny at the time, of course, but it's funny when you tell it . . . you see . . . you think about it, and things like that . . . oh, the things like that, you know, what you did
45 as kids . . . aye . . . er . . . and you're in a field, like, and I remember my

brother . . . we were caught redhanded in this field, you know . . . what
are you doing in here? Well, my brother just looked and says, what's up
with you, he says, this is Farmer Budd's field . . . we had no idea who
Farmer Budd were or not, you know, but this chap thought . . . he were
50   er just . . . er . . . a chap that was keeping us out, you see . . . that were a
funny incident, afterwards . . . it wasn't at the time . . . you know, our
Clifford had just the presence of mind to say . . . make out that he knew
the farmer, which we didn't . . .

Notes

1   Past tense of BE is *were* (l. 15) for all persons.
2   *You were sat there* (l. 7) = *You were sitting there. I was sat, I was
    stood* are widely used in parts of the north and west of England rather
    than *I was sitting, I was standing.*
3   *he'd about* (l. 22). This is the full verb HAVE (see p. 25).
4   *the* may be /t/ (e.g. *to t'fire*, l. 41).
5   *always* (l. 5) is /ɔːləz/, a form found in other accents.
6   *kid* for *child* (l. 5) is colloquial and not restricted to any particular
    area.
7   *happen* (l. 25) = *perhaps.*

VII Liverpool

LANCASHIRE

Liverpool

Wallasey
Birkenhead　MERSEYSIDE

WALES　CHESHIRE

Map VII

The accent of Liverpool is limited to the city itself, to urban areas adjoining it, and to towns facing it across the River Mersey (although its influence may be detected in other neighbouring accents). While the accent is northern rather than southern in character, it differs in a number of ways from other northern urban varieties, including those of the rest of Lancashire, the county in which Liverpool stands. Some of the differences show the influence of the large numbers of Irish people, especially from Southern Ireland, who have settled in Liverpool over the last hundred years.

1　The Liverpool accent is northern in that:
    (a) There is no contrast between pairs of words like *put* and *putt*, both being /pʊt/ (WL 4, 5). There is no /ʌ/ vowel.
    (b) /æ/ occurs in words like *dance, daft* etc., which in RP have /ɑ:/ (see p. 28; WL 21–6).
    (c) Words like *book* and *cook* have the vowel /u:/ (see p. 28; there are no examples on the tape).

2　Unlike in other northern urban accents (but in common with Newcastle), the final vowel of words like *city* and *seedy* is /i:/ (see p. 30).

3　There is no contrast in Liverpool speech between pairs of words like *fair* (RP /fɛə/) and *fir* (RP /fɜ:/) (WL 34–7). The most typical realization of the vowel is [ɛ:], but other forms, including [ɜ:], are also heard.

4　(a) /p, t, k/ are heavily aspirated or even affricated (cf. Cockney, p. 41). Thus:
can't (l. 5) [kxɑ:nt]
straight (l. 11) [streɪts]
back (l. 16) [bakx]

    In final position, /p, t, k/ may be realized as fricatives [Φ, s, x].
    (b) Related to this phenomenon is the relative infrequency of glottal stops in Liverpool speech.

    (c) Between vowels, the first of which is short, /t/ may be realized as
        [ɾ]. This is limited to certain lexical items e.g. *matter, what, but,
        get* (e.g. l. 21, *got a job*: [gɒɾəjɒb]). This is a feature found in
        other parts of the north of England.

5   /r/ is usually a tap, [ɾ] (e.g. *three*, l. 1; *real*, l. 3; *cigarettes*, l. 6).
6   /h/ is usually absent, but is sometimes present (e.g. l. 39, *him and
    her*).
7   /ei/ and /ou/ are narrow diphthongs (WL 8, 40, 41 and WL 12, 38,
    39) (figure 4.9).
8   Initially, /ð/ may be [d] (e.g. l. 10, *there*: [dɛ:]).
9   (a) The suffix –*ing* is /ɪn/.
     (b) Words like *singer* and *thing* (see p. 34) have [ŋg]. A clear
        example, because it precedes a vowel, is *thing*, l. 18.
10 All the features mentioned so far have covered particular segments
    of speech. But there is another feature, velarization, which is
    present throughout Liverpool speech and which gives it a
    distinctive quality. Velarization is the accompaniment of other
    articulations by the raising of the back of the tongue towards the
    soft palate (as in the production of dark /l/). This may be recognized
    on the tape if the reader first attempts to produce it himself.

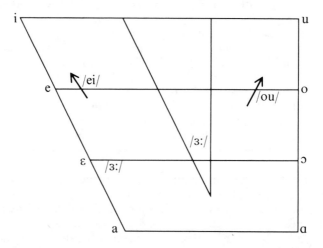

Figure 4.9 Typical realizations of certain Liverpool vowels

The recording

The speaker is a middle-aged barmaid who has lived all her life in
Liverpool. She talks about pubs she knows, and people who work in
them. The word list reader is younger and has a less pronounced accent.

Yeh, she's gone to America for three weeks, so we all go sad again
next week . . . she comes over . . . I'll go polishing everything next week
. . . she's a good manager, like, isn't she? but er . . . she's a real Annie
Walker, you know, everything's got to be so . . . she's . . . once you get to
5 know her, she's great but you can't drink and you can't have a smoke . . .
we're all walking round with four lighted cigarettes in our hand and
having a drink off everyone that gives us one . . . yeh, we're in charge,
yeh . . . well he's . . . he's er in charge of them all and I'm the monitor . . .
I'm er . . . when he's not there I'm in charge . . . but er it's . . . I tell you
10 what, if she left I wouldn't go out there . . . cos, you know, I do really like
working for her. She's straight . . . and she trusts you and that's imp . . .
that's the main thing, like, isn't it, you know . . . she is . . . she's great . . .
I don't think she's ever laughed till I went there . . .
   Course as I say, when you do your work you don't need erm a boss, do
15 you? that's what I say . . . this . . . this manager's made up . . . he said erm
. . . he's never co . . . he'll give us the tills, then he comes back about four
o'clock, and we've all locked up and gone . . . everything for him . . . he
says, one thing about it, he says, I haven't got to stand over yous . . . only
the night time, you know . . . course, where it is, of a night they have a lot
20 of er, you know, some that'll come a couple of nights, all these part-time
students . . . and some of them . . . er . . . got a job . . . going to Spain and
then want a few bob extra and then they just leave it. I don't know
whether they tap her till or what they do, but . . . he has to be there for
them of a night time . . . yeh, but it is, it's er . . . and it's a pub that you
25 wouldn't be frightened to bring anybody into, isn't it? . . . you know, it's
beautiful . . . er yeh . . . true yeh . . . oh yeh, you say . . . I say bye-bye in
there, I say tarrah up here . . .
   Mind you, she'll be round there drunk now if you went into the
Winifred for a drink . . . but I've never seen barmaids like them. They go
30 round well away shouting and everything and . . . and the boss and the
manageress is standing watching them . . . but they must be all right,
kind of thing, or otherwise they wouldn't put up with it, would they, like
. . . true, yeh . . . well, this is it . . . mind you, there's been three man . . .
three managers er sacked from there for bad takings . . . so they can't be
35 er all that good . . . and two of them is two that's been through each . . .
one that's, you know, er been sacked . . . yeh, that was [*name
erased*] . . . but then, after that there was erm a stout one named Jean
. . . and John . . . she was er an Australian, I think yeh, and she was here
that long waiting for a place that I took her in for three weeks . . . him
40 and her . . . and they were . . . she was a great person . . . I was made up
because I didn't take no rent off her, Stan, cos . . . I was . . . every
hafpenny she had had gone . . . paying for storage of furniture and she
had dogs and . . . all er so I just let her live here, like, but she used to have
a catering there as well, like Mrs Crighton. When I come home I'd have a
45 three course dinner, and I couldn't leave a handkerchief down it was

washed and ironed. I was made up because I didn't have to do nothing to help her . . . but, anyhow, it . . . he finished up erm . . . er . . . a night watchman on Runcorn bridge . . . that's the only place she could get a house was Runcorn . . . but it was a shame, though, with the money she 50 had and she was in . . . born in New Zealand and . . . everything and her staff pulled her right down . . . it is . . . she said to me, she said, Bridie, she said, they didn't take it in handfuls, they took it in fistfuls . . . and she was a real good manager t . . . to them, you know, you know especially Christmas, she wouldn't buy them er a box of handkerchiefs, something 55 like that, it'd be a suit . . . or a dress . . . and buy all their children, but yet they done all that on her like, you know, yeh . . . wouldn't be Mrs Crighton . . . she'd only l . . . find her once and that would be your lot, you'd be through the door.

Notes

1   There is multiple negation (see p. 13):
   I didn't take no rent off her (l. 41)
   I didn't have to do nothing to help her (l. 46)
2   (a) Past tense of COME = *come* (l. 44).
   (b) Past tense of DO = *done* (l. 56; see p. 15).
3   *yous* (/juːz/ when stressed, and /jəz/ when not stressed) is (often plural) *you*. It is a feature too of some Irish English.
4   The speaker makes a distinction between *bye-bye* and *tarrah*, both meaning *goodbye* (ll. 25–6). She uses the former in settings which she regards as socially superior.
5   *Annie Walker* (l. 3) is a well known television character, the manageress of a pub who is strict with her staff.
6   There are some perhaps unfamiliar lexical items:
   made up (l. 15) = very pleased
   tap (l. 23) = take money from
   well away (l. 30) = decidedly intoxicated
   where it is (l. 19) = the thing is
7   *like* (l. 3), *you know* (l. 4), *kind of thing* (l. 32) are best regarded as colloquialisms.

VIII Newcastle (Tyneside)

Map VIII

The speech of Newcastle is representative of that of the towns on and around the River Tyne. Some features of Tyneside speech are similar to those of Scottish accents (see next section).

1 (a) As in other northern English accents, pairs of words like *put* and *putt* are not distinguished, /ʊ/ occurring in both (WL 4, 5; see p. 27).

but

   (b) The final vowel in words like *city* and *seedy* is /i:/ (WL 19, 20; see p. 30).

   (c) As has been seen, /ei/ and /ou/ are wide diphthongs in the south of England, narrow diphthongs further north, and monophthongs in northern Lancashire and Yorkshire. On Tyneside they may be either monophthongs, [e:] and [ɵ:] or opening diphthongs, [ɪe] and [uo] (figure 4.10; WL 8, 40, 41, 52; 12, 38). But notice that *roll* (l. 58) has [ɔu]. The monophthongs would seem to be more prestigious realizations of these vowels, and are used by the reader of the word list, whose accent is not as broad as that of the other speaker (even taking into account the fact that he is reading carefully).

2 (a) Again as in other northern accents, words like *dance* and *daft* have /æ/ (WL 22, 23).

(b) Words like farm and car have /ɑ:/.
(c) Words which have /ɔ:/ in RP are divided into two sets in Tyneside speech.
   (i) Those which have *al* in the spelling have /a:/ e.g. *talking* (l. 56), *called* (l. 11), *all* (l. 53).
   (ii) Those which do not have *al* in the spelling have /ɔ:/, as in RP (WL 18, 33, 44, 45; *morning* (l. 17).
(d) Words which have /ɜ:/ in RP have /ɔ:/ in a broad Tyneside accent. So, *first* (l. 10) and *shirt* (l. 33) are /fɔ:st/ and /šɔ:t/, homonyms of *forced* and *short*. Notice that the reader of the word list does have the vowel /ɜ:/, at least when reading, and would distinguish between *first* and *forced*.

By comparison with RP, the accent of Tyneside lacks one vowel, /ɜ:/, but has one extra, /a:/. Correspondences between the pure vowels we have mentioned can be represented as follows:

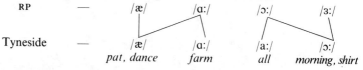

```
RP        —    /æ/        /ɑ:/        /ɔ:/        /ɜ:/

Tyneside  —    /æ/        /ɑ:/        /a:/        /ɔ:/
              pat, dance  farm        all      morning, shirt
```

3 (a) Word final *-er(s)* or *–or(s)* is [ɐ(z)] (figure 4.10; *tanner*, l. 4).
   (b) /ɪə/ is [iɐ] (figure 4.10; WL 14; *here* (l. 3)).
   (c) /ʊə/ is [uɐ] (figure 4.10; WL 42).
4 /ai/ is [ɛi] (figure 4.10; *right* (l. 46). (The word list reader's realization of this vowel is similar to that of RP speakers.)
5 /l/ is clear in all environments (cf. p. 51; WL 27–31).
6 /h/ is generally present.
7 *–ing* is /ɪn/ (*shilling*, l. 2).

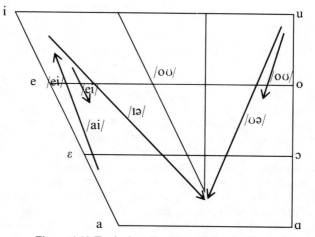

Figure 4.10 Typical realizations of certain Tyneside vowels

8   Between vowels, /p, t, k/ are accompanied by a glottal stop. *city*
(WL 19) is [sɪtʔiː]; *happy* (l. 29) is [hapʔiː] (see p. 30).
9   (a) Words which in RP have /au/ may have /uː/ e.g. *about* (1.4), *out* (1.6; see p. 71).
(b)   (i) *knows* is /naːz/ (see line 32 for contrast with *nose*); *though* is /ðaː/
(l. 38).
(ii) *was*, when stressed, is /wæz/; *what* is /wæt/; *who* (l. 63) is /we/.
(iii) *no, do* (l. 29), *nobody* (l. 63) have /e/.
(iv) *long* (l. 66) is /læŋ/.
(v) *father* (l. 64) is [fæðɐ].
10   In parts of Northumberland and Durham (but not very frequently
in Newcastle), /r/ may be uvular (the production of the sound
involving tongue and uvula, rather than tongue and alveolar ridge).
The recorded speaker's /r/ is variable. An example of uvular /r/ is
found in *remember* (1. 11).

The recording

The speaker is a man of about fifty who has lived almost all of his life in
and around Newcastle. His accent is quite strong. He talks about the old
days.

I'll tell you what, I often tell it at work. You know, they'd say to you,
'Hey, Jimmy, lend us a shilling, man'. What? Lend us a shilling . . . me
and I'd say to them come here a minute I'll tell you. I says, I can
remember when I used to shove a bairn about in a pram for a tanner a
week. Lot of money a tanner then a week. And I says, I've been pushed
for money ever since, so they divn't come back. Put them out the road.
Wey lad, get away, go on. Aye, he says, for a tanner. By, you can do a lot
with a tanner. You can gan to the pictures, get yoursel a penny fish and a
haipeth of chips, by God, yeh, and maybes a packet of Woodbines for
10 tuppence, and a match in, for to get your first smoke . . . bah . . . I once
ge . . . remember getting some Cock Robins, called them Cock Robins,
bah . . . they cock-robinned me, I'll tell you. I was at Newburn Bridge
. . . that's it . . . you can see Newburn, it's across there and I was smoking
away, faking, you know, instead of just going ph ph . . . swallowing
15 down, you know, I was sick and turned dizzy. I didn't know what hit us
with these Cock Robins . . . bah, but they they were good ones . . .
This old woman says to me one morning . . . Sonny . . . Sonny, why
you never said sonny them days you know. She says, would you like to
run a message for Mr Penn and for me. I says, yes I will do. She says, go
20 up to the shop and get him an ounce of tobacco. Oh, I says, thank you
very much, so I gans twaddling up the shop. When I gans back she give
us thruppence, mind thruppence, you know, that's about forty, forty-
two year ago, you know, Reg. Thruppence then was a lot of money. I

was there every day knocking at the door to see if she wanted any more
25 messages. Aye thruppence. Wey lad, ay, I'm getting thruppence off that
woman. What for? Wey, getting some baccy. Well, lad . . . Thruppence?
What a lot of money that was. Oh dear me, oh, we used to do such things
then, y . . .

We used to do some queer things then, but we were happy, man, aye,
30 we were happy. Once a rag man says to me . . . Hey sonny . . . What? . . .
He says, your hanky's hanging out . . . hanky . . . wey, you never had a
hanky then. You used to wipe your nose like that, you know. It was my
shirt tail hanging out of a hole in my pants . . . aye he says . . . your
hanky's hanging out. Well you never had a hanky then. Bah . . . you
35 used to gan to school. They used to line you up at school there. You want
a pair of shoes, I think. You want a pair of shoes. Wey, you never seen
them, you know, it was just a day out from Durham County for somebody from Durham down the road. Them were the days, though . . .

Then I went from there . . . and there's a house up there just beside
40 those two wireless poles. I went from there to there, and then I went and
got married and went and lived in with Florrie, and er I was like a bit
gypsy, I was in Blaydon first and Greenside I was, in Blaydon and
Greenside. That's what the doctor says. He says, Jimmy, you've a little
bit gypsy in you. He says we divn't know where you live. Then I shifted
45 from there to Crawcrook and from Crawcrook to Blaydon, aye, that's
right, aye . . . we sold the house at Crawcrook and I went to Coventry,
and when I come back I stopped with Florrie, and then I got a council
house into here. I've been in here about twelve year in. Oh, if I gan out
here I gan out with a stick, George, a stick in a big box, that'd not be very
50 long would it the box, about five foot ten, that the measurement of us.
When I get stiff, when I gan stiff about five foot ten . . .

But you used to get summers, didn't you. Wey, you used to get the
winters and all, pet. Oh, dear me, ow the winters. You couldn't stand the
winters now . . . yous lot couldn't stand it, could they? Course we used to
55 get the grub, you know. There was a fellow . . . there was a fellow at er
. . . when I'm talking about grub . . . he used to make leek puddings,
you've heard of leek puddings, you know . . . but he used to make them
about a yard lang, see, and put the leek in, and roll the leek up, see, just
like er a sausage, see . . . and this fellow was sitting, Japer Newton they
60 called him, he had about four sons and a lass, like, and he was sitting at
the end of the table, like . . . all sitting with our tongues hanging out, you
know, George. He was sitting at the end with a s . . . a big leek pudding.
He says, er, who wants the end? So nobody spoke, see, so he says again,
who wants the end, you buggers; Ted says I'll have the end, father, so he
65 cut the bugger in two. Aye, he cut it in two, a great big leek pudding
about a yard lang, cut it in two . . .

Notes

l. 2   *us* = me (also l. 15).
l. 3   *I says* see p. 17.
l. 4   *bairn* = child (in Scotland too).
l. 4   *tanner* = six (old) pence (not limited to Tyneside).
l. 5   *I've been pushed for money*: I've been short of money.
l. 6   *divn't* = didn't, don't, or doesn't (also l. 44).
l. 7   *Wey:* exclamation common on Tyneside.
l. 8   *gan* = go (also l. 35).
l. 9   *a haipeth*: a half pennyworth (not limited to Tyneside).
l. 9   *maybes*: maybe.
        Woodbines: once a common and inexpensive brand of cigarettes.
l. 10   *for to* = to (also found in Scottish and Irish English.)
        Bah!: exclamation not limited to Tyneside.
l. 17   Note the two pronunciations of *sonny*, the first being an imitation
        of the woman's accent, which he clearly thinks was 'posh', RP or
        something approaching it.
l. 18   *Them* is used as demonstrative adjective.
l. 21   *give* as past tense of GIVE (see p. 15).
l. 22   *thruppence* = three pence (not limited to Tyneside).
l. 26   *baccy*: colloquial form for tobacco.
l. 31   *hanky:* colloquial form for handkerchief.
l. 36   *seen* as past tense of SEE (see p. 15).
l. 37   *Durham County* = Durham County Council.
l. 38   *Them* as demonstrative pronoun (see p. 18).
l. 47   *come* as past tense of COME (see p. 15).
l. 48   *twelve year* see p. 19.
l. 53   *pet*: term of endearment much used on Tyneside.
l. 54   *yous* = you (cf. Liverpool, p. 64).
l. 55   *grub* (colloquial) = food.
l. 60   *lass* (northern and Scottish): girl.
l. 64   *bugger*: term of (often friendly) abuse, common in most parts of
        Britain. But also a 'taboo' word.
l. 65   *bugger* here refers to the pudding.

IX Edinburgh

Map IX

The vowel systems of Scottish English accents are radically different from those of England, and it is therefore not so helpful to describe them in terms of differences from RP. Scottish standard English speakers most usually have vowel systems approximately as given below (with words in which these vowels appear).

/i/	bee beer seedy meet meat			/u/	pull put boot poor
/e/	bay plate weight their mate	/ɪ/	pit bird fir city	/o/	pole boat board nose knows
/ɛ/	pet fern there	/ʌ/	putt fur	/ɔ/	cot caught paws pause paw pot Paul doll
		/a/	bard hat dance daft half father farther		
/ai/	buy	/au/	bout	/ɔi/	boy

It will be noted that:

1   Vowels such as RP /ɪə/, /ɜ:/ do not occur. This is because Scottish accents have preserved post-vocalic /r/ (see p. 31), the loss of which in RP led to the development of these newer vowels. Pairs of words like *bee* and *beer* (WL 7, 14) thus have the same vowel, but are distinguished by the presence or absence of /r/. The /r/ is normally a tap (see p. 51) but may also be a frictionless continuant.

2   Pairs of words such as *cot/caught* (WL 32, 33), *pull/pool* (WL 27, 28), *Pam/palm* are not distinguished (chapter 3). Length is not generally a distinctive feature of Scottish vowels. Monophthongs are 'pure'— there is no trace of diphthongization.

3   For many Scottish speakers, words such as *fern, fur, fir* have different

vowels. Different accents differ as to how far they preserve this distinction (WL 34, 35, 36).

4 A distinction is made between pairs of words like *tide*: *tied* (WL 46, 47), *booze*: *boos*, the second vowel in each case being longer. The basis for the distinction is that the second word in each pair has a word-final vowel plus an inflectional ending: *tie* + *d* (cf. London *pause*: *paws*, p. 40).

5 A distinction is made between pairs of words like *which* /hwɪč/ and witch /wɪč/. /hw/ is usually a single sound [ʍ], a voiceless [w].

The accents we have chosen to represent Scottish English come from Edinburgh (except for the word list—see below). While there are considerable differences between Edinburgh speech and the speech of other Scottish cities, the accents are sufficiently similar to act as a good guide as to what to expect in Scotland in general. In listening to less prestigious accents of Scottish English than that normally used by Scottish standard English speakers, the following points should be noted.

1 /ɪ/ and /u/ may be central [ə] and [ʉ].

2 /u/ may often occur where RP has /au/: *house*, for instance, may be /hus/, and is often written as *hoose* in Scottish dialect literature. This vowel, until a linguistic change (known as the Great Vowel Shift) which has taken place since medieval times, was originally found in these words in all varieties of English. In most varieties of English this vowel gradually became diphthongized from [u] TO [əu] to [au]. Many Scottish accents have not participated in this change (*down*, l. 50; *about*, l. 59; *round*, l. 60; *couch*, l. 82; cf. Tyneside, p. 67).

3 Instead of having *coat* /kot/, *cot*, *caught* /kɔt/, as described above, the urban accents of Edinburgh and Glasgow may have *coat*, *cot* /kot/,

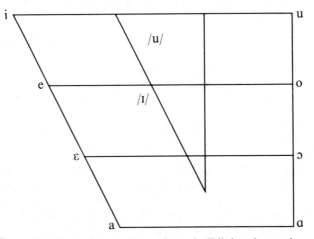

Figure 4.11 Typical realizations of certain Edinburgh vowels

caught /kɔt/. In these accents, that is, *socks* and *soaks, not* and *note* may be identical e.g. *box* (l. 72).

4   A number of words, such as *home, bone, stone, no* (which have /o/ in more educated speech) and *do, to* (which have /u/) have /e/ in very many regional Scottish accents (l. 85 *going to* /gone/; p. 72 *stones* /stenz/ l. 70).

5   In many Scottish accents many words such as *arm, after, grass* may have /ɛ/ rather than /a/ (*after*, l. 88).

6   The glottal stop is a frequent realization of /t/ (see p. 34; *better*, l. 20; *that*, l. 10).

7   /h/ is present.

8   *–ing* is /ɪn/.

9   A specifically Edinburgh feature is the pronunciation of /θr/ as in *three, through* as [ɹ�r̩]-it makes *through* sound very like *shrew* (*three*, l. 59).

The recording

There are three main speakers on the tape. The word list reader is from Glasgow and is at present studying at an English university. Although her accent clearly identifies her as Scottish, it is by no means strong.

The second speaker is from Edinburgh, and his accent is rather stronger, (e.g. he has glottal stops representing /t/ between vowels—but notice that house is /haus/). He talks about a certain area of Edinburgh as it was when he was young.

The third speaker is an Edinburgh schoolboy with a strong accent (e.g. *out* is /ut/). It will probably be very difficult to understand what he says, but we have included it, at least in part, to show how different from RP a regional accent can be. The boy talks first about gang fights and then about a film he has seen.

They were high tenement buildings and er many er sub-let houses, you know, broken up er bigger houses into . . . the room and kitchen was about the average house in these days, what we called the room and kitchen . . . with perhaps a toilet inside or outside on the landings . . . but
5   there was no such things as bathrooms . . . in these days in these areas, you know? . . .
Adam Street, which was in the centre of that area there was some very very good houses, rather old-fashioned but quite good houses with fairly big rooms and that, and these were sort of better class people er people
10   with maybe . . . s . . . minor civil servants and things like that . . . you know, that had . . . be able to afford dearer rents and that in these days, you know. But the average working class man . . . the wages were very small . . . the rents would run from anything from about five shillings to seven shillings, which was about all they could have possibly afforded in
15   these days . . . you just had to er . . . so it didnr . . . it didn re . . . matter

how many a family you had . . . er if it was two rooms, well, Devil take
the hindmost . . . aye, you couldn't get out of your environment, you see,
you just had to suffer it and make the b . . . most of it . . . and they all
survived, that was the great thing . . . no . . . no . . . no I think they were
20 better fed than these days, you know, the . . . they used to . . . the quality
of the food was better, I think, and the meat . . . no, that's correct . . . it
was er . . . pretty coarse meal and all that sort of thing and everything
was much more er farm produce was much more naturally grown, and
things like that . . . so that . . . so there . . . there were very big families,
25 you know, there . . . the average family was n . . . nothing under five
children in a family . . . very very rarely . . . oh you'd have them anything
up to nines, nine in a family living in two rooms, there was no
segregation or anything like that. The only hope was that somebody
would get married or something like that, you know . . .
30 There were some great stories in that area, you know, there were some
really . . . people were . . . they were quite er amusing that er how they
overcame their difficulties, you know, with er . . . they could improvise
. . . er . . . I rember a very funny thing though I don't, I was quite young
at the time, but there was a place in the Pleasance, off the Pleasance,
35 called the Oakfield Court, and it was a very very rough quarter,
everybody fought with each other in . . . in circulation . . . er one fought
one one week or the other . . . it was just drink and a fight, you know, er
very clean fighting . . . that er when they got into a good mood, they had
what they called the party called the surpriser! . . . and they . . .
40 somebody took the bed down in one of the houses and er moved the
furniture out into the street and all that, and they got two or three bottles
of beer and had a party, and . . . er . . . they were very lucky if it lasted t
. . . er the fight started again . . .

[It is clear from the next recording that fighting still continues in
Edinburgh]
Yes . . . aw it's the gangs . . . they just fight with knives and bottles and
45 big sticks . . . and bricks . . . takes place over at the big railway over there
. . . yes . . . they've got a gang . . . they call it Young Niddrie Terror . . .
round here they call it Young Bingham Cumbie . . . and that's how it
starts . . . they start fighting . . . yes . . . and they fight with other yins,
they fight with . . . Magdalene . . . that's away along the main road there
50 . . . if . . . Magdalene's just down that road . . . yes . . . and they fight with
the Northfields . . . and they go away on buses . . . and go to a lot of other
places . . . to fight . . . aw . . . about sixteen and that . . . yes . . . yes . . .
don't know . . . no . . . yes . . . well . . . there's only one person that lives
round here . . . this part . . . and the rest are . . . some of them live away up
55 the road there . . . and they're all round the scheme . . . well . . . there's
one of them . . . he . . . he takes a lot of them on, he's right strong . . . aye
. . . well, they . . . they have nicknames . . . I forget his name but . . . his

nickname but . . . he is strong . . . he fights with all these others . . . he
takes about three on at a time . . . yes . . . yes . . . because he is big . . . aw,
60 the police come rou . . . round just . . . just when it starts . . . see
all the police at night, they're going round the scheme . . . making sure
there's no fights . . . and all the laddies just run away when they see the
police coming . . . yes . . . aye . . . they run away and hide . . . till they
think it's safe . . . not always . . . they take them away down to the police
65 station . . . well, if there's any serious . . . injuries on anybody . . . they'll
get put in the children's home or that . . . so if they're old enough they'll
get put there . . . no . . . only one person . . . that was Billy . . . he was
caught . . . just a couple of nights or so ago . . . yes . . . some of them . . .
some . . . aw, they usually . . . there's wee-er laddies than me that goes
70 round there and start tossing stones at the laddies round there. They
usually get battered fae them if they get caught
    and these two boys are taking this big . . . metal box thing . . . down to
this big lorry, and it's got a big, ken, they table cloths . . . and he gets . . .
Norman Wisdom hides under it . . . ken . . . and he's walking with it . . .
75 taking it into this room . . . and they're putting it in the corner . . . and
Norman Wisdom's in the corner and that . . . and he's hearing them
making a plan about tak . . . taking these secret documents . . . and he
goes like that . . . the docu . . . he sneaks out . . . tries to crawl away . . .
the boy does that . . . boy goes like that to him . . . ken, the boy's trying to
80 get out the window and Norman Wisdom won't let him and he goes like
that . . . [buf] right in his face . . . Norman Wisdom goes right over . . .
the . . . couch . . . and the boy gets up . . . and he goes like that right over
Norman Wisdom's helmet, bends all the helmet . . . Norman Wisdom
gets up . . . chases after the boy . . . the boy gets out a door . . . and
85 Norman Wisdom's going to go out, ken . . . and he opens the window . . .
cos . . . he thinks the boy went out of the window . . . sees this other cop
standing . . . he takes the boy's helmet off and puts this bashed yin on
him, shuts the window, puts it on and chases after the boy again . . .

Notes

1   In the speech of both the man and the boy, *with* is consistently /wɪ/
    (e.g. l. 44). In more prestigious Scottish speech, *with* is /wɪθ/ rather
    than /wɪð/.
2   *all* is /a/ (e.g. l. 55).
3   Niddrie (l. 46), Bingham (l. 47), Magdalene (l. 49), and Northfields (l.
    51) are areas of Edinburgh. We do not know the meaning of Cumbie.
    (l. 47). *The scheme* (l. 55) is the housing estate.
4   (a) *yins* (l. 48) = ones.
    (b) *right strong* (l. 56) = *really strong* (this use of *right* is found in
        the north of England too).
    (c) *laddies* (l. 69) = boys.

(d) *ken* (l. 73) = know; its use here is equivalent to *you know* in other English dialects.

5 *this* and *these* with time reference may be found in Scottish English where *that* and *those* are used in standard English English (l. 3).

6 *they table cloths* (l. 73) = those table cloths (cf. p. 19).

7 *fae* (l. 71) = *from*.

X Belfast

Map X

In the northern part of Northern Ireland speech is quite similar to that of Scotland, which is where large numbers of settlers to Ulster came from. In the south of the province, on the other hand, speech derived originally from that of the West Midlands and the southwest of England. Belfast speech combines features from both north and south.

1   As in Scotland, there is post-vocalic /r/ (see p. 31). /r/ is realized as a retroflex, frictionless continuant [ɹ]. It is similar to word-initial /r/ in RP, except that the tip of the tongue is pulled back somewhat further.

2   (a) The vowel system is similar to that of Scottish accents:

/i/	bee beer seedy meet meat			/u/	put boot pull pool poor	
/e/	bay bear plate weight mate	/ɪ/	pit fir bird city fern fur	/o/	boat board pole knows nose pour pore	
/ɛ/	pet	/ʌ/	putt	/ɔ:/	Paul paw doll pause caught	
		/a/	pat bard hat dance daft half father farther	/ɒ/	cot	
/ai/	buy tide tied	/ɑu/	bout	/ɔi/	boy	

(b) Vowels are short before /p, t, k, č/, long before other consonants or when final.

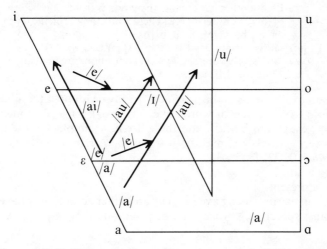

Figure 4.12 Typical realizations of certain vowels in Belfast speech

(c) In Belfast speech the actual realization of a vowel may vary considerably according to the sound which follows it. For example, /a/ in *daft* has a realization not very different from /ɑ:/ in RP, while in *bag* it may be [ɛ] (figure 4.12). Since the vowel in *beg* may also be [ɛ], the two words may not always be distinguished. This raises the question of whether it would be better to consider the vowel in *bag* to be /ɛ/ rather than /a/. For various reasons we have chosen not to do this, but the reader should be aware that the analysis of vowels could have been somewhat different from the one we propose (cf. /e/ v /ɛ/, and /o/ v /ɔ:/).

(d) The following notes on vowels should be read in association with figure 4.12:

    (i) /u/ is central, [ʉ].

    (ii) /e/ is normally realized as a diphthong varying between [ɛə] and [iə], but in words like *bay* (WL 8) and *say* (l. 12) the vowel is a monophthong, [ɛ]. In plural and possessive forms of these words, too, the vowel is [ɛ] (e.g. *days*, l. 48), and *days* therefore contrasts with *daze*.

    (iii) /ɪ/ is fairly central, [ɪ]. Although *fir*, *fur*, *fern* and *fair* may sometimes have different vowels, they all tend to be pronounced with [əɹ] which is probably best analysed as /ɪr/.

    (iv) /ɔ:/ and /ɒ/ contrast only before /p, t, k/, as in *caught* and *cot* (WL 32, 33).

(v) As has been mentioned above, realizations of /a/ may vary considerably. Before certain consonants (e.g. /f/ and /s/ in *daft*, WL 23, and *class*, 1. 20) there is a back or central realization. Before other consonants the vowel is front, and before /g/ and /ŋ/ may be raised to [ɛ]. (There is no example on the tape with /g/ or /ŋ/, but *back*, 1. 10, is [bæk]).

(vi) /ai/ is variable, but is often [ɛɪ] (WL 9, 46, 47).

(vii) /ɑu/ is very variable. Typical realizations are [æʉ] and [ɛi] (WL 13; *house*, 1. 1; *down*, 1. 5).

3   In some rural areas of the province, /j/ may be found after /k/ and /g/ before front vowels in words like *car*, [kjaɹ]. This phenomenon is only vestigial in Belfast, and there are no examples on the tape.

4   Between vowels /ð/ may be lost, so *mother* may be [mɔ̈:əɹ] and *another* (1. 22) [ənɔ̈:əɹ].

5   –*ing* is /ɪn/.

6   /h/ is present.

7   Certain words which have /ʊ/ in RP and other accents may have /ʌ/ in Belfast speech: e.g. *wood* may be pronounced [wʊd] or [wʌd].

The recording

The main speaker is a middle aged woman with a distinctive Belfast accent. The man who asks her questions is younger, and his accent is less broad. The woman talks about her past and about the fighting in the city.

    . . . born in this house . . . and still in it . . . Raymond
——You were born in this house?
I was born in this house, yes . . . b . . .
——So then you haven't lived in any other parts of Belfast, just this part.
5 Oh, aye . . . when I was about eight years of age my mother went down to the Ormeau Road to live, in Parscoe Street. But then . . . you see my Uncle Tommie's lived here, and his wife died . . . and he got married again, my mother come back to my granny . . . her . . . er mother and we've been there ever since again, that was in . . . during the . . . the war,
10 1941 or something we come back here, you know. So, counting all round, we weren't so long on the Ormeau Road, really, you know. I'd say about ten years, maybe twelve years, you know, no longer.
——And where have you worked in Belfast? What different places?
Well that's the only place I've ever worked in, Raymond.
15 ——In where?
Oh, aye, when I come out . . . when I was a wee girl of fourteen I worked in a . . . in a boot repairer's shop . . . they sold shoes and stuff too, but mostly repair work they done. Well I stuck it for a couple . . . for a year or so, and then, when I was about sixteen or so, my grandmother

20 got me into a place called Carsons, a very high class bakery shop, opposite the City Hall . . . that's gone, like, completely now, but . . . I done another couple of years there, then they closed up, there were two old sisters owned it really, you know, they were coming up to retirement age, really, and they . . . they sold their business then, you see, so . . . I
25 wasn't out of work that long until another lady got me into Inglis's . . .
——But, wh . . . when the sort of troubles were at their height recently, there was a lot of gunfighting around that area . . .
    Oh there was
——Now could you . . . was there any time when you yourself were sort
30 of . . . er . . . in danger around there . . . when you had any . . . can you remember any time when . . . you were frightened.
    Well I wouldn't say in danger, really, Rust . . . er . . . Raymond . . . we heard shooting and all going on when we were in work, you know. W . . . we had a window just looked out on to Eliza Street . . . and our
35 cloakroom, as we call it . . . when we used to hear the gunfire we used to look out . . . which is a very dangerous thing to do really, you know. Well then they had a gun battle . . . Belvoir . . . at the time of the Internment . . . remember the time of Internment . . . there was trouble down there really, you know, and . . . er . . . they'd lifted some people
40 that . . . old people and all, like old men that they had a grudge against that they shouldn't have lifted really, you know what I mean? And . . . er . . . it was just stonethrowing and troops and one thing and another, and a bit of . . . it went on all day. Well then there was a gun battle started on top of Inglis's . . . it's a flat roof Inglis's.
45 ——And you were working in the place at the time?
    No we were . . . funny enough, we were o . . . I was off on a week's holiday . . . then when Internment started, you know . . . but . . . em . . . I think they had to close up for a couple of days, really, you know, until it died down but there was a fellow, one of the terrorists was shot on the
50 roof, really, you know . . .
——Yeh, did you know any of the people that you knew in Inglis's who . . . sort of . . . were shot or anything like that or had er . . .
    No, only just round about that didn't work at Inglis's, really, you know, the time the Republican er . . . remember the time they had a . . . a
55 bit of a feud between the two sides. Republican and the . . .
——The Provisionals?
    Aye . . . it was the Provisionals and another . . . with Bernadette Devlin was over . . . now there was . . . the initials, I just can't remember, the initials, you know what I mean, Social something, you know . . . just
60 forget what the initials . . . well they had a bit of a go at each other, you see, and there was shooting and . . . I remember one time when I was in work at that time . . . and erm . . . everybody was lying low at the time, you know, I mean they all disappearing . . . I think half of Inglis's disappeared for a few days, even the security man disappeared . . . they

65 were all went . . . aye . . . y'know and then in a few days time when it was
all over they all come trotting back again . . . you know, you don't know
who . . . who was who, you know what I mean.
———But were you never afraid, like, in the middle of winter going
down there . . . an . . . you walked down there, didn't you? It must have
70 been dark in the early mornings or evenings coming back . . . it's a
dangerous place to go now at night, isn't it . . . I mean some people
wouldn't want to go there.
    Yes, I know, well . . . I never thought of danger, really, you know what
I mean, it never struck me . . . you know.
75 ———I mean, some people wouldn't walk in that area.
    That's right, I know . . . I remember one day there was shooting all
round over something, I don't know what it was . . . oh . . . down all the
streets there was shots getting fired here, there and everywhere . . . and at
about five o'clock I was coming home and it was pretty sh . . . pretty
80 dark, you know, and I saw this yellow car sitting up Cromac Street, and
a fellow over the bonnet of it . . . I said that's very like Harry Short's, you
know, anyway when I got up it was Harry Short . . . and all the shooting
was going round him . . . and there was Harry, his car or something had
went wrong and he was . . . says I, Harry what are you doing here, says I,
85 you could be shot, says I, you're . . . leaning over your bonnet fixing your
car . . .
———What did he say to that?
    He laughed hearty at the idea . . . well he had to get a tow home by the
RAC . . . something went wrong where he couldn't start his car . . . he
90 seemed to be . . . he didn't know that the shooting was going around
him, he was that interested in his car getting started . . .

Notes

1 (a) *come* (l. 8, 10, 16, 66) is the past tense of COME (see p. 15).
   (b) *done* (l. 18, 22) is the past tense of DO (see p. 15).
   (c) *went* (l. 84) is the past participle of GO (see p. 15).
2 *says I* (l. 85), see p. 17.
3 *hearty* (l. 88), see p. 19.

Suggestions for Using the Book

In what follows we assume that the reader has a copy of the tape which is available with the book. If he has not, we would urge him to obtain one, as its possession will increase significantly the value of the book to him.

The suggestions that we make are addressed primarily to teachers, but the individual reader, working through the book on his own, can also benefit from them. If he thinks of himself as both teacher and student, he should be able to do most of the exercises that we suggest, checking his understanding against our transcripts and analyses.

Just what is done with the book and recordings will depend on among other things the standard of English of the learners and on the use to which they intend to put their new knowledge. For this reason alone it is impossible for us to say what *should* be done. What we can do, however, is to suggest what *might* be done, based on our experience of using these materials with students of various backgrounds. Instructors can then select from our suggested exercises, modify them, and doubtless add to them, in whatever way they feel is appropriate to their particular teaching situation.

1 Reading

Chapters 1 to 3 can be given as reading assignments and used as a basis for discussion. The subject matter of chapter 1 in particular always seems to provoke lively argument. Reading and discussing chapters 2 and 3 is useful in that differences between particular varieties encountered in chapter 4 and on the tape will be seen as part of the more general differences outlined in these earlier chapters.

2 Comprehension

Most students in our experience are attracted by the challenge of trying to understand the tape recordings. But it is important, we think, that the task set them should not be beyond their ability. The instructor will have to decide how much information and other help he needs to give to particular groups of students. There is no need to use the recordings in the order in which they appear on the tape. As can be seen, we have made a geographical progression north and then across to Ireland, and in general the accents tend to become increasingly different from RP.

This does not take into account, however, the broadness of accent of our speakers. For example, the Bristol speaker (who has not such a strong accent) may be easier to understand than the speaker from London (whose accent is quite strong), even though, phonologically at least, London speech is closer than Bristol speech to RP. Almost certainly the most difficult recording for everyone will be the one of the Scottish schoolboy.

Students can be given a recording, or part of a recording and be required to:

    (a) give the general sense of what they hear;
    (b) answer comprehension questions set by the instructor;
    (c) transcribe orthographically passages from the recording. This exercise compels the student to concentrate hard and makes him recognize just what he does and what he does not understand.

3 Analysis

In trying to understand what is said, presumably the learner must carry out some kind of informal analysis. But as an activity in itself, analysis probably best follows comprehension exercises.

    (a) The instructor can ask for general observations on the accent (grammatical and lexical matters are perhaps most usefully treated separately).
    (b) Then a check can be made to discover how general the noticed features are and whether they form part of a pattern.
    (c) The analysis arrived at in the class can be compared with ours. Where there are differences, the recording can be examined for further evidence.

        The stage at which the word list recordings are introduced into these activities will presumably depend on the nature and level of the students concerned, as well as on the time available.
    (d) For some students it may be appropriate to attempt phonetic or phonological transcriptions of the tapes.

4   The recordings at the end of the tape are intended to allow the reader to test his ability to recognize and understand regional speech. This exercise should be kept until all the transcribed and annotated recordings have been worked through. Students may be asked to identify the accent and justify their choice. They can also be asked to transcribe the recordings.

Additional recordings

The recordings at the end of the tape are provided to allow the reader to test his ability to recognize and understand regional speech. The recordings are in the following order (we have inverted the script so that the reader should not learn the order by accident before attempting to identify the accents):

Norwich; Bristol; Bradford; West Midlands.

The northeast; Scotland; London; Belfast; south Wales; Liverpool;

Further Reading and References

Further reading

For a detailed description of RP the reader is referred to Gimson (1980). For an account of changes in the English language, see Strang (1970). Brown (1977) and Crystal and Davy (1975) (with which a tape recording is available) describe how normal English conversation differs from the careful style of English with which students are usually most familiar. Wells (1970) and O'Connor (1973) provide detail on British accents. Wakelin (1972) gives an account of rural accents and dialects.

References

Brown, G. 1977: *Listening to Spoken English*, Longman.

Crystal, D. and Davy, D. 1975: *Advanced Conversational English*, Longman.

Giles, H., Ball, S. and Fielding G. 1975: 'Communication length as a behavioural index of accent prejudice', *International Journal of the Sociology of Language* 6, 73–81.

Gimson, A. C. 1980: *An Introduction to the Pronunciation of English, 3rd edition*, Edward Arnold.

O'Connor, J. D. 1973: *Phonetics*, Penguin.

Palmer, F. R. 1974: *The English Verb*, Longman.

Petyt, K. M. 1977: '*Dialect*' and '*Accent*' in the Industrial West Riding, Reading University, unpublished Ph.D thesis.

Strang, B. M. H. 1970: *A History of English*, Methuen.

Trudgill, P. 1974: *The Social Differentiation of English in Norwich*, Cambridge University Press.

—— 1979: 'Standard and non-standard dialects of English in the United Kingdom: problems and policies', *International Journal of the Sociology of Language*.

Wakelin, M. F. 1972: *English Dialects: an Introduction*, Athlone Press.

Wells, J. C. 1970: 'Local accents in England and Wales', *Journal of Linguistics* 6, 231–52.

Index

Note: Because Scottish and Irish English vowel phonemes cannot be compared directly on a one-to-one basis with English English equivalents, they have not been included in the index. The reader is referred to sections IX and X of chapter 4 (pp. 70–79).